FOC

GROUNDS
FACT BOOK

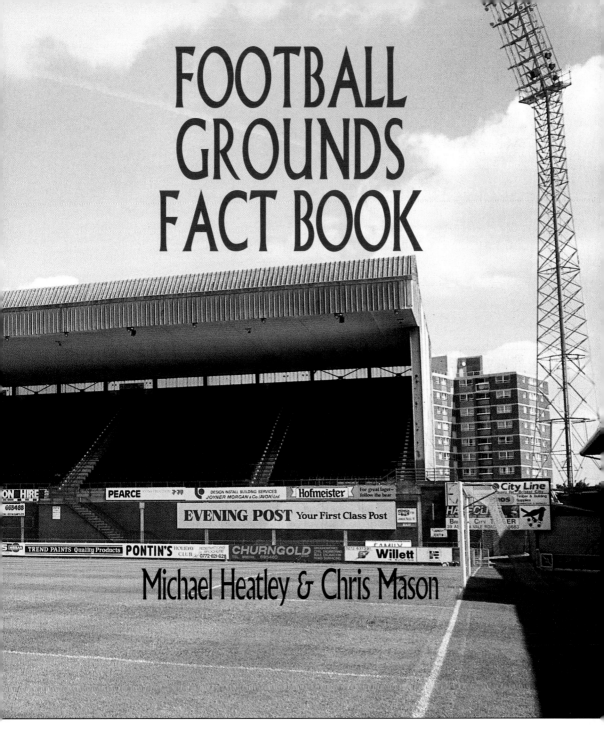

FOOTBALL GROUNDS FACT BOOK

Michael Heatley & Chris Mason

Ian Allan
PUBLISHING

First published 2004

ISBN 0 7110 3020 0

Published by Ian Allan Publishing

an imprint of Ian Allan Publishing Ltd, Hersham, Surrey KT12 4RG.

Printed in England by Ian Allan Printing Ltd, Hersham, Surrey KT12 4RG.

Code: 0411/E

Contents

The futuristic Millennium Stadium has helped to regenerate the heart of Cardiff. Events like the FA Cup Final have also been a boon to the city's economy. *HOK*

Introduction

Exactly a decade ago, one of the co-authors of this book traced with Daniel Ford in the book *Football Grounds Then And Now* (Dial House, now out of print) the changing shapes of British football grounds on a club-by-club basis. Even then, just two years after the Premier League and Football League had parted company, the landscape had started changing with an unfamiliar rapidity.

The twin horrors of the 1985 Bradford fire and Hillsborough four years later had led the powers that be to commission the Popplewell and Taylor Reports to provide a safe way forward for the game. No one, it was rightly argued, should leave home on a Saturday and contemplate never returning. Old structures

Below: **The way we were: a typical terrace crowd watching top division football in the 1960s.** Ken Coton

Right: **Ageing architecture: firemen inspect Crystal Palace's Main Stand for wind damage before a match, 2004.** *M. Heatley*

and practices were deemed no longer acceptable, while new stands and grounds were re-evaluated to cater for a breed of fan light-years removed from the cloth-capped blue-collar workers of yore. Or maybe it was the costs associated with these improvements that priced the old fans out of the market...

Whatever the reasons, the rate of change has accelerated since 1994. Of the clubs covered then, Bolton, Derby, Middlesbrough, Northampton, Southampton, Stoke, Sunderland, Reading, Manchester City and Leicester have moved into new stadiums. Bristol Rovers have returned 'home' and bought the Memorial Ground from the rugby team they moved in with, Brighton have similarly moved back to their home town and the temporary sanctuary of the Withdean Athletics Stadium, while Fulham are once more at their spiritual home, Craven Cottage – again, however, on a temporary basis.

opposite goal to the North Stand, houses away fans and now looks somewhat out of place.

Plans are in place for eventual additional tiers to the East Stand, which would increase capacity by 5,000 seats, and for the Jimmy Seed (South) Stand, developments which would raise overall capacity to around 36,000. No time scales for these proposed developments have yet been announced, however, and retention of the club's Premiership status would clearly be crucial. While Charlton's average attendances have risen satisfactorily from 19,558 in 1999–2000, their last season in Division One, to 26,256 in 2002–3, it's sobering to recall the record Valley figure of 75,031 recorded in an FA Cup fifth round tie against Aston Villa in February 1938. Ah, the good old days!

Above: **One of the unsung heroes who keep British stadiums fit and functioning.** *Ken Coton*

Left: **Sheffield United's Bramall Lane ground in 1995 – no longer three-sided.** *Robert Lilliman*

Standing, Sitting, Safety

Association Football has long been the world's most popular game, but for almost a hundred years little real concern was shown for the safety of spectators. A number of serious incidents occurred over the years, examples being the collapse of a wall at Sheffield Wednesday's Hillsborough ground in 1914, causing injuring to 80 people, and a man dying in a crush at Burnley's Turf Moor in 1924. There were countless other accidents at British football grounds, some of a far more serious nature (as will be seen later in this chapter) and, as football became even more of a world

game, tragedy also struck abroad: seventy-five fans were died in a crush at a first division game in Buenos Aires in 1968, while in the Soviet Union, a reported 340 people were crushed to death towards the end of a European Cup match between Spartak Moscow and Haarlem in 1982.

Although from time to time committees were formed and reports were written, little was done to ensure greater safety for spectators in

Crowd scenes from the 1967 Fulham v West Ham fixture. *Ken Coton*

on television. And what horrific viewing it was. City fans already knew that their team had won the Third Division championship, and their game against Lincoln City was meant to be a celebration, rather than the scene of a dreadful catastrophe.

Shortly before half-time, a fire broke out in Bradford's Main Stand, which had been erected as long ago as 1908. The likely cause was a cigarette end or lighted match, which had been dropped through a gap in the floorboards. This had then ignited rubbish, which had apparently been accumulating in an inaccessible area beneath the stand for a number of years.

It was thought at first that the fire was a relatively minor incident and many supporters were at first reluctant to leave their seats. Flames could however be seen beneath the gaps in the wooden flooring, and so someone went in search of a fire extinguisher. Sadly, there was no fire extinguisher in that part of the stand, and within minutes the fire spread upwards and reached the wooden roof. The

roof, covered with tarpaulin and sealed with asphalt, was ablaze within seconds, and soon the entire structure was on fire.

Some people managed to escape onto the pitch, but others were far less lucky. Access from the rear of the stand was severely restricted and some exit doors were found to be locked or boarded up. There were many tales of heroism, and some people who might otherwise have died were rescued by other supporters. Even so, 56 people were killed. A national appeal raised £4 million for the families of the victims.

Heysel

In May 1985, when England, and much of Europe, was in the grip of so-called 'football hooliganism', Liverpool were playing in the European Cup Final against Juventus. The venue was the Heysel Stadium in Brussels, a crumbling edifice which was palpably unsuitable for the purpose, and which had in fact been condemned as a venue for major matches. Fighting broke out during the game, a wall collapsed and 39 people – mostly Juventus fans – were killed. As a result, English teams were banned from European competition for six years.

A 1971 match at Bradford City's Valley Parade. The wooden Main Stand in the background would be destroyed by fire 14 years later with great loss of life. *Ken Coton*

Laying Down the Law

Lord Justice Taylor made a total of 76 recommendations designed to improve the state of football in Britain in his 1990 report following the Hillsborough disaster. The most important of these were:

- The gradual replacement of terraces with seated areas in all grounds by the end of the century, with all First and Second Division stadiums being all-seater by the start of the 1994–5 season and all Third and Fourth Division by 1999–2000.

- Setting up a Football Stadium Advisory Design Council to advise on ground safety and construction and to commission research into this area.

- That no perimeter fencing should have spikes on the top or be more than 2.2 metres tall.

- Making ticket touting a criminal offence.

- Introducing new laws to deal with a number of offences inside football grounds, including racist chanting and missile throwing.

- Sending older offenders to attendance centres and using new electronic tagging devices for convicted hooligans.

Left: **Segregation is rare outside the League arena, but Witton used it when hosting Conference games for Northwich in 2003–4.** *M. Heatley*

Below: **Simple waist-high barriers are the norm at non-League grounds such as the Lawn, home of Forest Green Rovers.** *M. Heatley*

Hillsborough

Four years later, when Liverpool journeyed to Sheffield Wednesday's Hillsborough ground for an FA Cup semi-final against Nottingham Forest on 15 April 1989, tragedy struck once more. Once again, the event was witnessed by millions via their television screens. On this occasion, it was Liverpool supporters who were suffocated or crushed to death, when the police allowed too many people to enter the Leppings Lane end of the ground. Even before the game kicked off, it was clear to many that there was severe overcrowding at one end of the stadium, but still the fans piled in. By the time the referee abandoned the game, after just six minutes, people were climbing over the

Left: **An impressive cantilevered stand at St Johnstone's 10,700-capacity McDiarmid Park, 1990 has helped the ground host rugby internationals.** *Robert Lilliman*

Below left: **Southampton's 32,700-seater St Mary's Stadium is magnificent even when hardly occupied.** *M. Heatley*

Many clubs have, however, relocated. In the seven years between 1992 and 1998 no fewer than nine clubs moved, namely: Chester City (Deva Stadium), Millwall (New Den), Northampton Town (Sixfields), Huddersfield Town (McAlpine Stadium), Middlesbrough (Riverside), Derby County (Pride Park), Sunderland (Stadium of Light), Bolton Wanderers (Reebok Stadium) and Reading (Madejski Stadium). And there have been others since, notably Southampton (St Mary's), Charlton Athletic (back to The Valley), Leicester City (Walkers Stadium) and Manchester City (City of Manchester Stadium).

The clubs which were affected by the 20th century tragedies all have new or refurbished stadiums: Ibrox retains its listed red-brick façade, but the ground was mainly redeveloped during the late 1970s and early 1980s. Bolton

Wanderers have moved to the Reebok Stadium, the space-age design of which can be seen from miles around, while Bradford City's stadium, although having a somewhat lop-sided look to it, is also impressive, dominated as it is by the large and imposing Carlsberg Stand. At Hillsborough, Sheffield Wednesday, currently languishing in Coca-Cola League One, have four large two-tier stands and, while the ground has received less investment than some, it is still a fine-looking stadium.

So, where has all the money come from? The aforementioned Football Trust has provided some of it and John Major, while he was Chancellor of the Exchequer in 1990, announced that tax on football pools was to be cut by 2.5%, thus releasing £100 million over five years to help clubs redevelop their grounds. Sponsorship deals have also provided much needed revenue, and there has been an explosion on the marketing front. Clubs like Manchester United have a world-wide fan base which generates a great deal of money but

Huddersfield Town's impressive Galpharm (formerly McAlpine) Stadium, viewed from pitch level. *Robert Lilliman*

English, and to a lesser extent, Scottish, fans are also paying the price by way of increased admission charges. Football's finances are always precarious, but it does seem that out of the various disasters, dreadful as they were, has come a new and safer environment for all.

Footnote
Exeter Emergency
In 1999 there was nearly another crowd disaster, when Exeter City entertained Aldershot Town in an FA Cup second round tie. There were hundreds of Aldershot supporters

Chelsea's ground as it once was – Chelsea v Fulham, 4 March 1967. *Ken Coton*

still outside the ground at 3pm but no decision was taken to delay the start of the game. An exit gate was pushed in, and a few fans entered an already overcrowded part of the little St James' Park stadium. Fortunately, most of those outside the ground had enough good sense not to follow them, and a Hillsborough-type disaster was averted. This comparatively recent incident does, however, show that there is no room for complacency.

Safety First

Steve Cottingham, Farnborough Town's safety officer, outlines his matchday role:

'The job of safety officer at any football club is a very important one and, for certain levels of the national game, is required by law. There's lots of responsibility and some authority, but essentially it's about working with others at the club to ensure that whatever the attendance, people come and go safely – even the match officials!

'My interest in safety at football grounds came about through tragedy. I was at Hillsborough, the home of Sheffield Wednesday FC, for the FA Cup semi-final between Liverpool and Nottingham Forest in 1989 and, as a Liverpool supporter, I stood on the Leppings Lane terrace – thankfully for myself, not on the part where most were injured or died. It was what went wrong on that fateful day that provided the motivation for undertaking the role.

'There are essentially four parts to the job: pre-match communication and intelligence gathering; pre-match inspection of the ground; briefings for the chief steward and match officials; and follow-up after the match.

Pre-match Communication
'The general manager and I touch base to talk about the opponents' fans – how many are likely to travel and by what means. He usually finds this out when he contacts the opposition in the week leading up to the game. We also consider whether we need a police presence and whether to segregate the ground. Part of the job entails maintaining liaison between the club and local police. Occasionally I will speak to my visiting counterpart.

Pre-match Ground Inspection
'Usually undertaken about two to three hours before kick off, removing anything that could be considered dangerous or reporting anything that needs the attention of the Ground Development Association. The club's safety certificate demands that all areas are checked, including the dressing rooms, social club, hospitality areas and the tea bars.

Briefings
'With the pre-match inspection done, the next job is to brief the chief steward and matchday stadium manager on anticipated attendance of away supporters, means of transport and anything else that stewards might need to keep an eye on.

'Once spectators are admitted to the ground, the role is one of working with the chief steward and other stewards to ensure there are no problems during or after the match. I will also liaise with police if they are present.

'About an hour or so before the game, I report to the match referee and speak to him/her about the assistants, sometimes including the FA's referee assessor and brief them on emergency procedures, ground evacuation, etc.

Follow-up

'With the match over and people either safely on their way home or, better still spending their money in our social club, and, following a debriefing with match officials and any assessor, I can relax a bit. I check with the chief steward and general manager to see if there is anything that has arisen during the game that I need to deal with. On occasion I speak to the club chairman.

'The job doesn't finish with the end of the match. Once I am home, it's on to the Football Safety Officers Association (FSOA) website, where I file a report on the match: the final score, the attendance, how many opposition fans, how they travelled, whether the match was 'police free' and any problems encountered.

'The FSOA is a voluntary membership organisation consisting of all the safety officers for Premiership, Football League and Football Conference clubs. It is recognised by the Government and the various footballing authorities as the official voice for safety matters at football grounds. At this time it is regrettable that only eight out of 22 Conference clubs are members.

'Being in the FSOA allows me to tap into best practice and consult with qualified people on safety issues. For example, I recently attended a regional meeting at Swindon Town FC and met safety officers for Reading, Swindon, Portsmouth, Wycombe, Cardiff, Bristol Rovers and Plymouth football clubs, representatives of an associated company that provides trained stewards, as well as two officials for the Football Licensing Authority which governs safety issues for all affiliated football clubs in England and Wales. The FSOA also trains safety officers, which leads to a national (and FA) recognised qualification. It's what I aspire to achieve.

'I also write a report for the club, which is kept as a record that would, if necessary, be produced for the Safety Advisory Group (SAG). This is run by Hampshire County Council, the body that issues and oversees our safety certificate. I can report that county council representatives from the SAG attended a match recently and complimented our stewards who, when questioned by them on safety issues, clearly showed that they knew how and when to deal with particular types of incident.

'Although day-to-day responsibility for health and safety at the club must rest with the secretary/general manager, because I am a part-time volunteer, he and I consult each other on a regular basis on general health and safety matters within the club.'

Farnborough safety officer Steve Cottingham in light-hearted mood. *Panther Studio*

needing the largest, and most expensive, policing operation. Up to 400 police officers (perhaps costing more than £300,000 per annum) may be needed for a major Premier League fixture, while less than 30 may be required for some lower division matches. Mounted units and dogs are not normally used at these latter games. Each club pays for the use of police inside the ground under a Special Services Agreement. The clubs used only to pay a percentage of the cost, but now they have to bear the full cost of policing. This is one reason why many clubs, especially those playing in the lower divisions, now recruit a lot more stewards than they used to.

Local Difficulties

Derby clashes have traditionally aroused the fiercest passions among fans, and the Worthington Cup tie between near neighbours Watford and Luton Town in September 2002 saw a total of 20 people jailed for nearly 20 years and banned from all football matches for periods of up to seven years after crowd trouble both inside and outside Watford's Vicarage Road ground.

Kick-off had to be delayed when supporters fought running battles on the pitch after around 50 Luton fans jumped advertising hoardings at the away end. At one point a supporter was seen to rip up a corner flag and brandish it like a weapon. One supporter was rushed to Watford General Hospital with a head wound.

Police eventually restored order by forcing the pitch invaders back into their seats and blocking off the area behind both goals. The kick-off was delayed by 15 minutes. Speaking after the sentencing, Senior Investigating Officer Steve Read said: 'This is an excellent result, and we hope it sends out a very strong message to others who are intent on causing violence at football matches. With the use of CCTV footage, the involvement of football intelligence officers, the support from both clubs and the co-operation of neighbouring forces we were able to collate a package of evidence in relation to the disorder. Working together we then went about putting names to the faces of those who had perpetrated the violence and conducted a series of arrests. We hope that our methods will now form a template for future investigations into football violence.'

Vicarage Road, Watford, scene of recent crowd disturbances.
Northdown

Arsenal stewards stand out from the crowd.
D. Heatley

Effective stewarding inside the ground usually means that fewer police officers are considered necessary. Stewards are cheaper than coppers, but in the last few years some concern has been expressed about the policy of clubs which employ a lot more stewards in order to save money. At some grounds, a rise in hooliganism has been detected, and in September 2002 serious questions were asked about the lack of policing at Watford's Vicarage Road ground, when a game against local rivals Luton Town sparked one of the worst outbreaks of unrest in recent years.

The clubs' Football Intelligence Officers are required to travel with the fans to away games. They are likely to know about any individuals who are suspected of organising, or being involved in, football-related disorder, and this information is shared across the football intelligence community. At home and away, the FIOs use intelligence and knowledge to identify those known to cause disorder. They effectively police the hooligans by shadowing them or controlling their movements: for example, by stopping them going into certain pubs or by insisting that they follow a certain route.

Since the Taylor Report and subsequent legislation, football clubs have had to take more responsibility for safety at their grounds. The clubs now place far greater emphasis on the training of stewards, although some employ outside agencies for their stewarding. Crowd control within the stadiums has been made easier with, for example, double barriers, walkways and family enclosures. Stewards can now obtain an NVQ Level 2 in Spectator Control, accredited by City & Guilds. This covers events such as pop concerts, as well as football.

Some clubs have been commended for their

stewarding. Leeds United, together with the company which provides their stewards, were amongst the first football clubs to receive an award for excellence in steward training. Meanwhile, Coventry City is ensuring its stewards will be fully prepared for the move to a new stadium in 2005, by joining forces with Telford College of Arts and Technology to ensure stewards are provided with the training they will need. Coventry has always taken stewarding very seriously, and it has some of the best-trained people in the country. Other clubs take note.

Left: **Warning notice at Gay Meadow.** *M. Heatley*

Right: **Police stand guard in front of a flooded stand in the 1970s.** *Ken Coton*

Below right: **Disturbances are not always confined to stand or terrace.** *Ken Coton*

Drunk and Disorderly?

Alcohol and football have made uneasy bedfellows for many a year now, and recent times have seen derby fixtures or those with a troublesome history moved forward to a midday kick-off to minimise pre-match drinking time. However, clubs make money out of selling booze, so certain conditions have been imposed to ensure that alcohol cannot be consumed while in view of the pitch. At Hereford's Edgar Street, this results in the clubhouse bar being shuttered during the 90 minutes of action.

Even so, all regular football fans must have had their enjoyment ruined by a drunk standing (or, even worse, sitting) in too close proximity to them at a match. The prospect of breath-testing supporters to establish their ability to watch a game was brought in for Euro 2004, with England fans the predictable guinea pigs. Sports minister turned media commentator David Mellor was incensed: 'As a catalyst for trouble this is a world beater,' he stormed. 'Think about it: the delays, the confusion, the anger of people excluded from a match they've paid to see.

'The basic principle is flawed, too. A lot of people watch football who are over the limit for driving but that doesn't make them either drunk or likely to behave badly. Dead drunk yobs are easy to spot without a breath test.'

The procedure also failed to counter the problem of fans, particularly 'corporate guests' of the sort encouraged by clubs to purchase entertainment packages, being plied with drink before and during games. This could lead to problems when such guests were seated within the home support, as happens at many UK grounds.

Above: **The existence of Premier League 'firms' is suggested by freshly daubed graffiti at Fratton Park, 2004.**
M. Heatley

Left: **Many clubs now contract out stewarding to specialist companies such as Goldrange.**
M. Heatley

Right: **Senior steward at Tamworth's ground – figures of authority should always be clearly recognisable.**
Northdown

Below: **The number of police at matches has declined since this 1970s crowd scene, largely due to clubs footing the bill.**
Ken Coton

The National Stadiums

Wembley, Hampden, Windsor Park and the Millennium Stadium

Wembley

By the early 1920s, with the ravages of the Great War still fresh in the minds of many, the English football authorities decided that the country's football-loving public needed a bit of cheering up. For once, they got it right. It had long been clear that England needed a national football ground, at which international games and FA Cup Finals could be played, and now there was to be a brand-new stadium which would soon become synonymous with the game. A site was selected at Wembley, just northwest of London and, once construction began, the stadium was completed in record time.

And what a place it was. There were colonnades and arches, an art deco-style banqueting hall and, above all, two massive towers which would soon be recognised all over the world. The Empire Stadium (as Wembley was officially known) was the most spectacular football ground on earth. It could accommodate in excess of 100,000 spectators and it was not long before its capacity was to be put to the test as, just a few days after the construction work was completed, Wembley was to host the 1923 Cup Final between Bolton Wanderers and West Ham United.

The 1923 FA Cup Final could well have ended in disaster. The match was organised by the British Empire Exhibition authorities, rather than by the Football Association itself and, unbelievably, it was not an all-ticket affair. The likely attendance was seriously underestimated,

Wembley Stadium in 1978 as so many football fans remember it, albeit with a sparse crowd for the 1978 FA Vase final. *Robert Lilliman*

The legendary twin towers which are being replaced in the new Wembley by a proscenium arch. *Robert Lilliman*

appearance of Police Constable George Scorey and his horse, Billy. The first Wembley Cup Final is remembered as the 'White Horse Final' although Billy, white though he looked, was in fact a grey.

Nobody was killed at Wembley's first football match, but the FA decided that, in future, it would stage all Wembley matches itself – and its cup finals would be all-ticket affairs. At least it got that right. The Empire Stadium was the venue for the Empire Exhibition of 1924, for the Olympic Games of 1948, and of course for England's finest hour – the 1966 World Cup Final. In its later years it was also the venue for large-scale music events – notably the Live Aid concert of 1985. Wembley has, however, always been primarily associated with the Cup Final. 'Getting to Wembley' was the ambition of every football club, large and small, after that first final, even though the stadium gradually became run down and most people realised that it would one day have to undergo serious refurbishment, or perhaps even be completely rebuilt.

Wembley continued to stage the FA Cup Final until the end of the 20th century, when it was decided that, even though by now it had been converted into an all-seater stadium, the old place would have to go. Many football enthusiasts throughout the world felt that this was a bad decision, and one that would long be regretted. It was hoped at first that at least the famous twin towers would be saved, but in the end it was decided that they could not be incorporated within the new design. The saga of the new Wembley Stadium has been a long and complicated one. Political wrangling and accusations of financial mismanagement dogged the scheme in its early days, and more

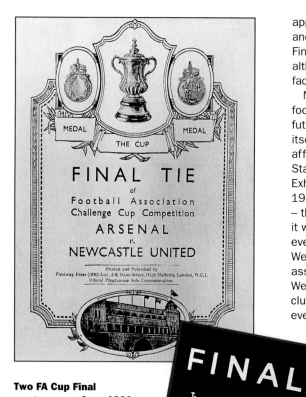

Two FA Cup Final programmes, from 1932 and 1936, both of which incorporate the Wembley Stadium silhouette.
Northdown

and about a quarter of a million people turned up in the hope of gaining entry. Quite a lot of them did get in, by the simple expedient of climbing over the wall. The official attendance figure was 126,047 but it is anyone's guess just how many fans actually got into Wembley on that historic day. Spectators spilled out onto the playing area and the game was delayed while dozens of policemen tried to push them back. It all seems to have been done with remarkable good humour and the game is famous for the

Wembley's seating, seen during the 1988 League Cup Final, was not universally praised by supporters. *Graham Betts*

than two years passed before the old Wembley was finally demolished.

The twin towers are no more. In their place is a vast construction site, with a new state-of-the-art stadium gradually beginning to take shape. When it is completed, sometime in the year 2006, it will have 90,000 seats (more than 18,000 of which will be reserved for corporate entertainment), a steel arch reaching to a height of 133 metres which will support the sliding roof, two giant TV screens for action replays – and 2,000 toilets. Very nice. The stadium will also be used for Rugby League and athletics events, and for anything else which is likely to bring in a lot of money. High revenue will be important, as the stadium is costing an incredible sum: in the year 2000 the total cost was estimated at £485 million, but the final bill is now likely to be well in excess of £700 million. Architect Sir Norman Foster's vision will be turned into reality by an Australian construction company, and will be partially financed by a German bank. Approximately £170 million of public money is going into the scheme, a large proportion of which is 'Lottery Money'. Unbelievably, an estimated £82 million is going on fees for lawyers and bankers.

The area surrounding the new stadium will be subjected to 'regeneration' and the provision of up to 2,000 new homes, some offices and shops, and the inevitable 'leisure facilities' which people will be told they need in order to improve their quality of life. It's beginning to look as though it will turn out all right in the end, and it is to be hoped that Wembley Stadium will once more come to be regarded as the spiritual home of football.

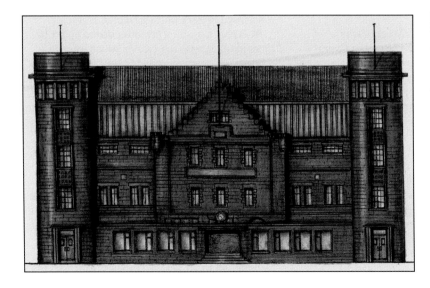

Hampden

The story of Hampden Park is really quite remarkable. Queens Park Football Club, which later made its home at Hampden and which still plays

The original Archibald Leitch-designed frontage of Hampden Park, home of Queens Park FC and the venue at which Scotland's internationals are staged. *Gerry Blaikie (www.scotcities.com)*

An empty Hampden Park, pictured in the 1980s before modernisation. *Robert Lilliman*

there in the Scottish Third Division, was founded in 1867. Five years later its players made up the entire Scottish side for their country's first ever international against England. Amateurism was the norm at the time but, as other clubs turned professional, Queens Park retained the amateur status which it maintains to this day. And so it is that one of Scotland's smallest clubs – and the only amateur side to play in either the Scottish or the English league – still occupies the vast open spaces of Scotland's national stadium, and regularly attracts several hundred spectators.

The stadium is, however, not as vast as it once was. It was built in Glasgow during 1903 and at that time had a crowd capacity of 80,000. The first match played there was between Queens Park and Celtic, a 1-0 victory for Queens Park which attracted a gate of 44,530. This was a low attendance figure by comparison with the crowds which were to attend matches in Scotland over the next few years, and it was soon clear that additional terracing was needed. It was duly constructed, and by 1910 the official capacity was raised to 125,000. It was further raised in 1927, by which time extra standing and seating space had pushed the figure to 150,000. In 1937 a Scotland versus England game, which Scotland won 3-1, attracted a crowd of 149,547.

Hampden Park was now a vast bowl and the 'Hampden Roar' was as famous as Wembley's Twin Towers – at least in Scotland. It certainly was quite a roar, and it must have been very intimidating for visiting players. Hampden continued to attract vast crowds, with 135,000 people attending the European Cup Final between Real Madrid and Eintracht Frankfurt in 1960. By the early 1990s it was however very apparent that Hampden was in serious need of upgrading, and so a redevelopment programme was put in place.

This started in 1993, with the reconstruction of the North and East Stands, which were followed, between 1996 and 1999, by the impressive new South (BT Scotland) and West Stands. There were of course financial problems. There always are. The third phase of the redevelopment was put on hold in the year 2000 but by this time Hampden had already been transformed into a 52,000 capacity multi-functional stadium. In May 2001 the Scottish Museum of Football was opened, and at about the same time the office accommodation within the National Stadium was completed. The Sport Medicine Centre was opened in April 2002. The total cost has exceeded £70 million, with £22 million coming from private sponsors.

There are complicated management and financial arrangements surrounding the new set-up at Hampden Park, but Queens Park Football Club are still there, and still get a few hundred people at their matches.

Windsor Park

Northern Ireland has never had a national football stadium of its own. For almost a hundred years, whenever an international venue has been needed, it has hired the Windsor Park Stadium in Belfast from Linfield Football Club. As a League ground, Windsor Park is perfectly adequate, having four stands, two of which were constructed within the last decade or so, and a capacity of just over 20,000. As an international venue, however, it falls short of today's high standards. An example of its basic problems came in September 2003 when, following Northern Ireland's game against Armenia, even the toilet facilities put in place for players to provide urine samples were deemed to be inadequate.

Northern Ireland is as football mad as any other country in the United Kingdom, a fact which is hardly surprising when one considers some of the great players that have come from the province, and it would be a great shame if Windsor Park were to be struck from the approved international list. In recent years, some of Northern Ireland's international matches have attracted small crowds, but during 2003 there was much concern over the poor facilities available for the 2006 World Cup qualifying games – particularly those against England and Wales. In November 2003 UEFA issued a warning to the effect that, if the sub-standard facilities were not improved, Windsor Park's future as an international venue would be in severe jeopardy. This would mean that games would be taken out of Northern Ireland altogether.

A few weeks after the warning from UEFA, Michael McGimpsey, a former Northern Ireland sports minister, called for public money to be made available to help the stadium meet the necessary standards. Meanwhile, the general secretary of the Irish Football Association was also calling upon the Government to take action. However, at the time of writing (May 2004) this situation was still unresolved.

The Millennium Stadium

'We're on our way to Cardiff, we shall not be moved' does not have much of a ring to it, and most English football fans were horrified at the announcement that, for the time being at least, the FA Cup Final would be played at Cardiff's new Millennium Stadium. In 2000 Chelsea beat Aston Villa by a goal to nil in the last Wembley Final. The crowd numbered 78,217, it was a fairly turgid game, and there wasn't a white horse anywhere to be seen. Nevertheless, this was a nostalgic occasion and it was the end of a very long era. In 2001, the Final would be played in Wales.

The Millennium Stadium proved, in fact, to be a very fine place for a cup final, which is perhaps all the more surprising when you consider that the site was once the home of Glamorgan County Cricket Club. The new stadium replaced Cardiff Arms Park, which itself was built on the site of an impressive 17th century town house close to the River Taff. Glamorgan played cricket there between 1921 and 1966, after which work began on the building of the National Rugby Stadium. Glamorgan had never been the most successful of county cricket sides, allegedly because the Cardiff Arms Park pitch was often a little on the damp side.

Views inside and outside of Cardiff's new Millennium Stadium

Above: **Cardiff Arms Park was the venue for Wales' international matches until supplanted by the Millennium Stadium.** *Robert Lilliman*

Right: **Far from causing problems, the inner-city setting for the futuristic Millennium Stadium has helped to regenerate the heart of Cardiff. Events like the FA Cup Final have also been a boon to the city's economy.** *HOK*

The newly constructed Cardiff Arms Park had a crowd capacity of 53,000, including 11,000 places on the terraces. Work on it began in 1967, but it was to have a comparatively short life. Wales was soon to need a more up-to-date national stadium, which would be capable of hosting football, rugby and anything else which attracted a large crowd. The city of Cardiff was busy shedding its image as a dreary dockland town, whose only known claim to fame was that it had been the birthplace of Shirley Bassey, and becoming a regenerated, vibrant and cosmopolitan city. Doubts were expressed about the Millennium Stadium when the plans were first drawn up, but as the edifice rose towards the sky, it could be seen that this was something just a little bit special.

Work began in 1996, with the hosting of the 1999 Rugby World Cup very much in mind. There were the usual delays, problems and missed deadlines, and the final cost was in the region of £134 million. There were fears that the enormous, largely steel, construction would prove to be an overpowering presence, but the use of colour on the exterior walls has a pleasing effect and lessens the impact of the sheer size of the building. The stadium has its now-famous retractable roof, which means that never again will games be postponed due to inclement weather. It is situated near to the railway station in the city centre, and it has a seating capacity of around 74,000.

By common consent, Cardiff's Millennium Stadium is currently the finest in Britain and when the new Wembley is finally finished, it seems that the United Kingdom will at last have a few stadiums to rival the best in Europe and beyond.

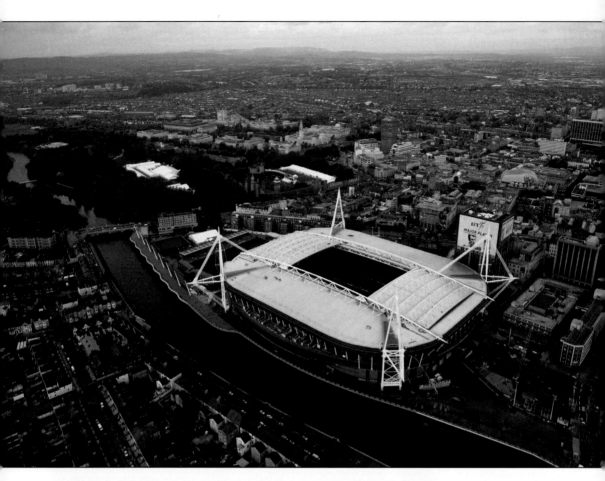

As well as murals, the interior of the Millennium Stadium has been decorated by paintings of celebrated Welsh internationals like Ryan Giggs, Ian Rush and Gary Speed.

HOK/Pippins Design

Away From Home

Every now and again a football club deserts its traditional home in favour of a new stadium. There have been a number of such relocations in the recent past, and the reasons for moving vary from club to club. During the 1980s and 1990s many of our older grounds were deemed to be outdated, and unsuitable for modern day football and modern day supporters. Some clubs, like Manchester United and Aston Villa, were able to effect major improvements to their existing stadiums, while others, like Middlesbrough and Reading, decided there was insufficient room to reconstruct and expand, and so they sought pastures new.

Inevitably, some supporters resist these changes, even when the economics make good sense for the clubs concerned. In many cases, however, supporters not wishing to see their club move from its traditional home have failed to put up much of a fight – principally because they were in a minority. This has often been the case with smaller clubs like Northampton Town, whose move to the smart little Sixfields Stadium on the edge of town in 1994 was seen by most supporters as a fresh new beginning for a club run on a shoestring budget. And, when Mr Madejski offered them one, how could Reading supporters resist the idea of a brand-new stadium to replace the crumbling edifice of Elm Park?

It is the enforced relocations, loved by nobody, that spur supporters into action – with varying degrees of success.

Happy Valley

Charlton Athletic supporters have always shown total dedication to their club, and to its home at The Valley in London

SE7. In 1919 the early supporters of the Southern League club dug out a chalk pit to form what was to become one of England's largest grounds – with a capacity of more than 75,000.

Charlton's ground was seldom full, and the club was never a large one when compared to its then near neighbours Arsenal. Even so, the Addicks thrived, being elected to the League Division Three (South) in 1921 and eventually, in 1936, gaining promotion to the top division – where they failed by only three points to win the League title at the first attempt.

By 1985, however, Charlton Athletic's halcyon days seemed to be well and truly over. The club had suffered financial problems since the 1950s, but by the mid-1980s new safety legislation meant that The Valley was considered unfit and unsafe for spectators. A great deal of renovation work would be necessary to bring the stadium up to the required standards, but the money for this work was simply not available. And so, in September 1985, fans entering the ground for a local derby against Crystal Palace were given a piece of paper informing them of the closure of The Valley.

The supporters had known it was likely to happen, but even so, the news came as a

The Valley falls into disrepair, 1985. *Robert Lilliman*

MESSAGE TO OUR SUPPORTERS

It is with regret that we must announce that we will be obliged to leave The Valley the home of Charlton Athletic Football Club for 66 years.

Recent events have forced this unhappy decision upon us. On 1st July the owners of the land behind the West Stand gave notice terminating our right to use or occupy the land. Court proceedings were commenced to evict and we have been obliged to agree to go by the end of September.

On 6th August 1984, the Greenwich Magistrates ordered that the East Terrace be closed as work was required to the concrete steps and crush barriers. We were not informed of defects to the crush barriers when we were given an opportunity to take a lease of The Valley literally two hours before we appeared before the High Court Judge in March 1984 to obtain consent for the arrangements to save the Club.

The facilities at The Valley for the safe and orderly entrance and segregation of fans and accommodation for spectators and car parking have been so drastically curtailed by the effect of the two sets of court proceedings that we have had no alternative but to make other arrangements.

With effect from 5th October, the home matches of Charlton Athletic Football Club will be held at Selhurst Park which will be in future home for both Charlton and Crystal Palace who will keep their separate identities. We are delighted with this arrangement and the big welcome Crystal Palace Directors are giving us.

HOW TO GET THERE

BY BUS

No. 75. From Charlton Village to Selhurst/Norwood Junction (every fifteen minutes) — journey 50 minutes.

BY TRAIN

Charlton to Norwood Junction.
Change at London Bridge.
Charlton to London Bridge 2 trains every hour journey time 14 minutes.
London Bridge to Norwood Junction 3 trains every hour journey time 20 minutes.

The shaded part of the drawing below shows the land we cannot use as from 30th September 1985.

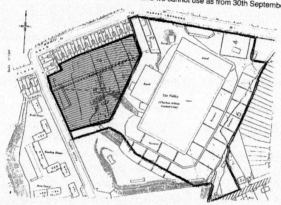

In the crisis we endeavoured to find a home in the London Borough of Greenwich, but although the Council was most helpful, to find even merely adequate facilities was impossible. Our players will continue to train locally at Charlton Park and our South Eastern Counties League matches will continue to be played at Meridan Sports Ground. It is still uncertain where we will play our home Football Combination Matches. It is our firm intention to make Charlton Athletic a First Division Club and we are delighted with such a good start to the season. Our big worry is the inconvenience which will affect you, our supporters, practically and emotionally. Like most of you I have been a supporter of Charlton Athletic for many, many years and feel very sad indeed at the prospect of football no longer being played at The "Valley", but delighted with our prospects at Selhurst Park.

We wanted you, our supporters to be the first to know. To help supporters who find it impossible to get to Selhurst Park we are prepared in the interim to provide a number of coaches. Please contact the Secretary if you wish to travel this way.

Season Ticket Holders will be offered the best seats in the house, with enormous regret, a refund, if they do not wish or cannot carry on supporting Charlton Athletic. We expect to be able to make special discount arrangements for people who wish to watch both Charlton and Crystal Palace first team games. A letter will be sent out soon to all season ticket holders.

Some compensation is that facilities at Selhurst Park are superior to those at "The Valley" and the playing field is in first class condition too.

Lets give the lads a bigger cheer this afternoon and encourage them to provide a result to take us nearer Division One.

JOHN FRYER

Above: **A leaflet handed to Charlton supporters in 1985 instructing them how to find their new home at Selhurst Park.** *Author's collection*

Right and far right: **Bristol Rovers' Eastville Ground in 1980 with the greyhound track clearly visible.** *Robert Lilliman*

shock. Ironically, it was at Selhurst Park that Charlton were to spend the next six seasons, groundsharing with Palace, before transferring for a single season to West Ham's Upton Park. Although at times the cause must have seemed a hopeless one, Addicks fans never gave up hope of returning home. After three years at Selhurst Park there appeared to be the chance of a return, and the supporters once more went along to The Valley, this time to do some much needed repair work. It was to no avail, as the old stands were still deemed to be unsafe.

Hopes may have been dashed, but the dedicated fans were not going to give up. They organised themselves and proposed the building of a new stadium on the same site. When Greenwich Borough Council refused planning permission, the fans formed their own political party and fought the next local election. The Valley Party campaigned on a single issue – the return of Charlton Athletic to its traditional home – and campaign posters began appearing all over the borough. When the votes were counted, it was clear that the party had been supported not only by Charlton fans, but also by ordinary people, who may not have been particularly interested in football, but who appreciated the justice of the cause. The Valley Party won almost 11% of the total vote.

The publicity generated by the campaign eventually caused the council to change its mind. In April 1991 it reversed its decision concerning planning permission and, 20 months later, Charlton Athletic were back at The Valley. The stadium's capacity is little more than a third

of that of the original ground but the club, currently playing in the Premiership, had scored a remarkable success – due almost entirely to the determination of its loyal supporters.

Early Bath
A year or so after Charlton moved out of The Valley, Bristol Rovers were forced to leave their Eastville home. The club had been there since 1897, the year in which they purchased the ground for £150. They owned it until 1940, when financial pressures forced them to sell it to a greyhound racing company for £12,000. However, Rovers continued to play at Eastville until mounting debts and an increase in the rent forced them to seek a groundshare with non-League Bath City in 1986.

Their new, shared, home at Twerton Park was barely adequate for Third Division football, but somehow Bristol Rovers survived. Their long-suffering fans were forced to endure regular journeys to Bath for many years, before a solution was eventually found. The supporters naturally objected to the situation, but many believed that a new home in Bristol would be forthcoming sooner, rather than later. But the years rolled by, and in the event it was 10 years before the Pirates sailed back to Bristol and a new home at the Memorial Ground.

Just for a change, they had to groundshare. This time it was with Bristol Rugby Club, but Rovers did at least own a 50% share in the stadium, for which they paid £2.3 million. When the rugby club later called in the receivers, the Pirates were able to buy their share for a nominal sum and they now own the ground outright. One more happy ending.

Wombling Free
The Wimbledon story is a confusing one, and it is hard to say where it will all end. For a while there were two Wimbledons, but now the original club is known as the Milton Keynes Dons.

Wimbledon does in fact have a quite remarkable history. The club from Plough Lane, London SW19, campaigned long and hard for

Above: **Bristol Rovers not only found a home at the Memorial Ground but ended up buying it from their landlord.** *Robert Lilliman*

Left: **Plans for the futuristic development at Severnside in the 1990s which would have incorporated a new ground for Bristol Rovers in a community sports centre. The scheme was abandoned.** *McAlpine/S. Arnold*

Below left: **Bath's Twerton Park played host to Rovers during their exile from Bristol.** *Robert Lilliman*

membership of the Football League. During the 1970s, supporters of the Southern League side placed little stickers in the back windows of their cars, bearing the legend 'Dons 4 Division Four' and eventually, in 1977, Wimbledon quit 'non-League' football in favour of the big time. The team had something of an up-and-down existence for a few seasons. Having twice been promoted to Division Three, and twice relegated again, the Dons eventually topped Division Four in 1983. At the end of the following season they were runners-up for the Third Division title, and found themselves

The Battles Continue

A London Assembly report called 'Away From Home' was published in June 2003. The report recommends that the Mayor's London Plan should outline the strategic importance of football clubs and their stadiums, and that football authorities need to be clearer about the sanctions available to them when faced with another 'Wimbledon'.

In recent years, many of the clubs which have faced extinction, or removal from their native territory, have been located in the London area or in the southern part of the country. This has been largely due to sharply rising land prices, but there are currently many League football clubs up and down the country which face similar problems. In the north of England, Oldham Athletic have been on the brink of bankruptcy for some time, while York City's Bootham Crescent ground has been sold by the club's ex-chairman for £3.5 million. With so much money going into the Premiership, and so little going to the clubs struggling in the lower leagues, many more fans are likely to be putting up resistance in the future.

about to do battle in Division Two. Just two seasons after that, they won promotion yet again and by season 1986–7 they were members of the First Division.

The tiny Plough Lane ground was never suitable for top-flight football, but that didn't prevent the Dons from finishing in 6th place in their first Division One season. It was a fairy-tale story, and it got even better when they reached the FA Cup Final in 1988 – and beat Liverpool at Wembley. The club held on to its top flight place, and became inaugural members of the Premier League in 1992. There was a certain amount of criticism of the

The first game of Wimbledon's 2001–2 season is greeted by black balloons at Selhurst Park.
Neil Presland

team's direct style of play, but it seemed the supporters would have the last laugh.

Sadly, though, the writing was on the wall, and Plough Lane was abandoned before the Premier League came into being. Wimbledon moved to a groundshare at Selhurst Park in 1991, following Charlton's move back to The Valley. Crystal Palace were happy to continue to share costs with another club, but Wimbledon's fans were far from happy. The

Hearts Transplant

In 2004, Edinburgh's Heart of Midlothian revealed they were to sell their current home, Tynecastle, and move to the city's Scottish national rugby stadium, Murrayfield. The club, presently £17 million in debt, believed it was the only way to secure its financial future.

It had received an offer for the Tynecastle site from a major residential and commercial property developer. 'The board has estimated an immediate potential financial benefit would be £0.8 million in the year ending July 31, 2005, as the result of net expenditure and interest savings following a disposal of the stadium for net proceeds of £12 million.'

But Hearts fans united to condemn the club's proposal to sell Tynecastle and move to Murrayfield and started working on their own rescue plan. There was resentment over chief executive Chris Robinson's plans, while an Edinburgh businessman offered to buy Tynecastle and lease it back to the club.

Hearts playing legend Gary Mackay was delighted to learn that the fans were rallying together on the issue, insisting it is the only way the Gorgie faithful can attempt to fight to save Tynecastle.

'I was absolutely delighted to see representatives of the three fans' groups come together as one voice,' he said. 'The only way forward for the support is with strength in numbers. And it was wonderful to hear they all agree with the sentiments surrounding the proposed move from Tynecastle. When I first spoke about this topic I was concerned about the apathy which was being shown by the fans but it's great to see them trying to do whatever it takes to ensure the move to Murrayfield doesn't happen. It is only right they give the management and players their 100% backing but the togetherness they are showing on the stadium situation is very encouraging.

'I have been a player and a supporter in times when there was disagreement with the way the club was being run, and I don't agree with these monumental decisions, which could affect the very existence of Hearts, being taken without due consideration to the views of the thousands of people who have followed the club through thick and thin over the years.'

John Borthwick, secretary of the Federation of Hearts Supporters Clubs, believes a move to Murrayfield would have a devastating effect on supporter numbers. 'I think it would be a death-knell for the club,' he said. 'Having spoken to Hearts fans this is the view I got. The Murrayfield capacity is 67,500 and they are talking of blocking off the top tier. Fine, but the capacity is still 37,000, twice that of Tynecastle. I think the Hearts fans will go along and be put off by the lack of atmosphere. I know Chris Robinson talks about supporting the team and not the stadium, but the two go together.'

The supporters remain 'unconvinced that the proposed sale of our only asset is a prudent way forward' since it robs the club of a valuable asset should Hearts slip into future financial disarray. 'While the club must be financially viable without relying on borrowing against our main assets, a contingency is required should past history recur,' the statement said. 'We also remain unconvinced that Murrayfield is a viable option and believe that a move there will decimate the fan base.' Hearts remain at Tynecastle for the 2004-5 season and the move to Murrayfield has been put on hold. The fans hope it will never happen.

club had always had a small fan base and the move to Selhurst Park, with its impossible parking facilities, caused many of its supporters to drift away. There were plans for a retail development at Plough Lane but, by 2004, a decision was made to use the site for housing.

Initially, supporters campaigned for a return to the old place or, if that was not possible, for a new stadium somewhere in the vicinity. But the seasons dragged by and, when chairman Sam Hammam sold the club in 1997, it soon

Wimbledon fans take their grievance to the Football League chairmen outside Carlton TV studios, 2002. *Neil Presland*

became clear that the new Norwegian owners had other ideas. Earlier rumours of a possible move to play in Ireland had come to nothing, but now it seemed the destination was Milton Keynes. Not quite so far, but far enough for the majority of remaining supporters to decide to form a new Wimbledon.

While the old Wimbledon Football Club, now known as the Milton Keynes Dons was beginning the 2003–4 season playing First Division football at Milton Keynes' National Hockey Stadium, AFC Wimbledon was embarking upon its second season in the Premier Division of the Combined Counties League. The new club had been unsuccessful in its attempt to join the Ryman League at the start of season 2002–3, but the team finished in third place in the Combined Counties and regularly attracted crowds numbering between 2,500 and 3,500.

The 2003–4 campaign saw AFC win 42 matches out of 46 and draw the remaining four, finishing on top of the league – 27 points clear of their nearest rivals. The AFC Wimbledon story is a remarkable example of what supporters can achieve and up to 1,000 of them regularly travel to away games, depending on the capacity of the grounds visited.

The new club resides at the Kingsmeadow Stadium in Kingston, Surrey, and hopes one

Milton Keynes' National Hockey Stadium in late 2003, not long after Wimbledon FC (now MK Dons) took up residence. *Robert Lilliman*

day to gain a place in the Football League. It has now progressed to the Ryman League Division 1.

Seagulls Over Kent

Brighton's problems are far from solved, although they do currently play in a stadium

not too far away from their traditional home. The club inhabited the Goldstone Ground for 95 years before, in 1997, it was forced to groundshare in the next county.

The sale of the Goldstone by majority shareholder Bill Archer and his chief executive, the sometime Liberal Democrat Member of Parliament for Eastbourne, David Bellotti, was the cause of widespread protest. For a time it seemed as if the team – which had taken Manchester United to an FA Cup Final replay just 14 years earlier – would fold, but Gillingham came to its temporary rescue and the Seagulls played at the Priestfield Stadium for two seasons. It is, however, a long way from Brighton to Gillingham, and the fans were far from happy.

A groundshare arrangement at the Withdean Athletics Stadium was eventually negotiated, but this could only be a temporary measure and the stadium remains unsuitable for their needs in many respects, not least because of its limited capacity. Indeed, managers Peter Taylor and Steve Coppell both left the club during its period of uncertainty for jobs they perceived had more potential. Taylor ended up at the palatial KC Stadium, Hull, prepared to sacrifice a rung of League status for the possibilities five-figure crowds could offer. Players, too, followed this lead with a detrimental effect on the club's progress.

There could scarcely be more difference between the cramped Withdean Athletics Stadium (above left) which Brighton now inhabit and the state-of-the-art Falmer complex (left) they seek to occupy. *BHAFC*

At the Withdean, an athletics track surrounds the pitch, the west end of the stadium remaining closed to spectators. A small North Stand is the stadium's only permanent structure. It is reserved for season-ticket holders but comprises only a few rows of seats, and these are at pitch level. Away fans use 400 temporary seats in the northeast corner next to the team entrance, a smaller block of temporary seating being situated in the southeast corner.

Brighton's temporary home came with many conditions attached. Limited parking in a wealthy residential area forced the creation of park-and-ride facilities (match tickets including two free travel vouchers for use on the bus) while no music can be played at the ground until 30 minutes before kick-off. Finally, tickets cannot be bought from the ground on a matchday even if available.

Over recent years, several sites in the Falmer area of Brighton have been suggested for a permanent 22,000-seater stadium, but objections from residents have always been forthcoming. In November 2001 700 supporters, including Seagulls fans Des Lynam and pop star Fatboy Slim, attended a campaign launch for a stadium bid. The pressure from supporters seemed by now to have worked and, in February 2003, a public inquiry was opened into the proposed building of a stadium at Village Way North, Falmer. This was referred to John Prescott in early 2004, when all English clubs showed commendable solidarity by each sending the Deputy Prime Minister a bouquet of flowers in their colours to support the bid. Brighton's play-off win against Bristol City appeared to give them even more ammunition.

Cottage Chronicles

Fulham's troubles began in earnest in 1986, when chairman Ernie Clay sold his interest in the club, and its Craven Cottage ground, to a property developer. Less than a year later the new chairman proposed a merger with Queens Park Rangers, with the new club to play at Loftus Road – a stadium owned by the same company. There was, inevitably, an outcry from the supporters of both teams, but for a time it seemed that Fulham Park Rangers really would come into existence.

Fulham fans began at once to campaign

Writing on the wall: Fulham redirect forgetful fans and give notice of redevelopment.
Northdown

against the proposal, beginning with a peaceful pitch invasion. Football people across the country were on their side and within a few months the plan was scrapped, with former Fulham player Jimmy Hill assembling a small consortium to take over the club. It seemed that Fulham was safe, but Hill's group had bought only the club – and not the ground. Over the next 10 years rumours of redevelopment of Craven Cottage abounded. There were plans for a partial redevelopment, changes of ownership of the land, plans for relocation, public inquiries and a great deal of confusion. An organisation called Fulham 2000 was set up to raise money, and although the response from Fulham supporters and many others was tremendous, it still seemed likely that, at best, the club would be forced to relocate. With no money to spend on players, Fulham had been sliding gracefully down the League, finally being relegated to the bottom division, and there seemed no way back. And then Mohamed Al Fayed came along.

Fulham had in fact – quite remarkably – won promotion back to Division Two in 1997. Perhaps this encouraged the Egyptian multi-

Rebuilding of the Hammersmith End (above) and Putney End proceeds at Craven Cottage, spring 2004. Across the river (below) the now all-seater stadium takes shape in preparation for Fulham's return for the 2004–5 season.
Kevin Freeman

millionaire to invest in the club, and invest he did. Fayed promised to build a state-of-the-art stadium at Craven Cottage, but his plans did not meet with the approval of local residents and, in any case, the new chairman eventually decided that the building costs would be too high. To his credit, he had spent a massive amount on players in order to achieve Premiership status. While the new stadium was still on the drawing board, Fulham moved to Loftus Road to groundshare with QPR on a temporary basis. The club returned to its attractively modernised stadium in the summer of 2004 but, apparently, the search for a suitable site for a new stadium continues. Fulham supporters had rallied to the cause with some success, but the long-term future of the club as a major force in English football is still uncertain, as it is for Craven Cottage itself.

The Ashburton Agenda

Arsenal's plan to swap Highbury, their home since 1913, for nearby Ashburton Grove is, after Wembley, Britain's biggest and costliest stadium development of the new millennium. Yet the fact the project has been beset with difficulty, again like the English national stadium, seems symptomatic of the challenges facing the game as a whole.

A successful club now makes more money from sources other than gate receipts: Arsenal's most recent accounts showed match revenue of £28 million dwarfed by TV income of £52 million, this having mostly been generated by participation in the Champions League. Critics claimed this proved clubs could earn more with a good team than a big stadium. So was the move five minutes (600 yards) 'up the road' really necessary when a redeveloped Highbury, with corners filled in and a new Clock End that formed a mirror image of the North Bank, would have upped capacity from 38,000 to not far short of 50,000?

Supporters of Ashburton Grove said that if the Gunners could not make a profit when they won the Double in 2002 they had no

The Clock End at Arsenal before seating and even protection from the elements, 1965.
Ken Coton

option but to relocate. Certainly, the plans for their proposed new home were nothing if not impressive. The 67,000-capacity stadium, designed by HOK Sport, Venue and Event Architecture, boasted four tiered stands and a roof design similar to another HOK project, the Stade de France in Paris. It would match Old Trafford in capacity, making the Gunners the major power of the south. (It is worth recording that Arsenal's record attendance at Highbury, 73,295 against Sunderland in March 1935, established in the 'standing' era, remains considerably in excess of Ashburton Grove.)

HOK Sport's chairman Rod Sheard declared that the project was 'a wonderful opportunity to design a world-class Premier League stadium in the context of the close urban fabric of north London. We are not trying,' he said, 'to build the biggest stadium in the world, nor are we trying to build the most expensive.

Highbury's East Stand, 1983. *Robert Lilliman*

What we are aiming for is to build the most beautiful stadium in the world.'

The move from Highbury, initially in time for the start of the 2005–6 season, was first announced by Arsenal in November 1999. A draft planning brief was approved for public consultation purposes by Islington Council the following January, and in November 2000 a planning application was submitted. London mayor Ken Livingstone smoothed the way by expressing his support.

Plans of the new stadium were unveiled, public consultation suggesting that 75% of Islington residents were in favour of the project. Planning permission was granted in December 2001, but two dissenting Islington residents took their case first to the High Court and then the Court of Appeal. This meant work on the new stadium stopped temporarily. The arguments they put forward were dismissed in late 2002, but the following April saw the club announce a year's delay in the completion of the stadium to August 2006.

Escalating costs had prompted speculation that the project could be abandoned but Arsenal had already spent £50 million on it. Their bankers, the Royal Bank of Scotland, struggled to arrange the £317 million needed to fund the project with the club nearly £45 million in debt.

The first steps had been taken in August 2002 when demolition work began at Lough Road, Islington, in preparation for the building of a new, state-of-the-art Waste and Recycling Centre. With this up and running, the current station housed on the Ashburton Grove site could shut down.

Funding for the stadium project was finally assured in February 2004 and construction work resumed at the new stadium site. Highbury itself would be redeveloped for housing, the four stands being used to house around 450 flats and the pitch remaining as a communal garden for their residents. Arsenal are (in summer 2004) as yet undecided whether to sell the site to a property developer or develop it themselves.

Highbury fills up to its 38,000 capacity in early 2004. *D. Heatley*

Computer-generated view of a match day at Arsenal's Ashburton Grove Stadium.
HOK Sport, Venue & Event Architecture

Archibald's Architecture

Archibald Leitch (1866–1938): Football's Architect

The second half of the 19th century was the age of the architect and engineer. Some, like Isambard Kingdom Brunel, built great ships and bridges, while others pioneered motorised transport or, like the lesser known Robert London, laid telegraph cables under the Atlantic Ocean. Scotland in particular was known for the inventive brilliance of its engineers, and one Scotsman, Archibald Leitch, became famous for the design of football stadiums.

Or rather, he didn't, because most people, even football fans, knew little or nothing about him. In more recent years it has, however, become clear that Leitch was an architectural pioneer, without whose efforts many grounds would have looked totally different. And the game of football would have been the poorer for it.

Archibald Leitch came into this world in Glasgow during 1866. An intelligent and practical lad from a middle-class family, he was a grammar school boy, and he later attended the Andersonian College. When he was 16, he became an apprentice at the engineering works of Duncan Stewart & Co of Glasgow. He was there for five years, gaining experience in engineering and draughtsmanship, before going to sea as an engineer. He later returned to Duncan Stewart & Co, as its superintendent draughtsman in the Marine Department, but this time he did not remain long with the old firm. Perhaps he already had another old firm on his mind, but for the present he was content to set up his own company and to concentrate on what would now be called consultancy work with various Scottish county councils and other public bodies.

The Old Firm's Architect

By 1902, Leitch was a full member of the Institution of Mechanical Engineers and it seems he was looking to break away from helping with the design of town hall buildings

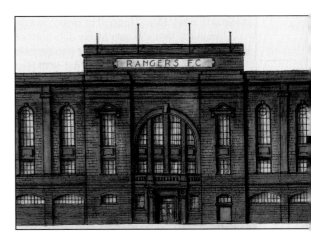

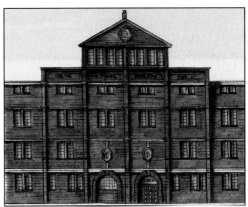

Leitch's immortal hat-trick of Hampden Park, Parkhead and Ibrox Park shaped the face of Scottish football. The artistry in designing the façades of Glasgow's Old Firm Rangers (top) and Celtic (above) is clearly visible in these sketches. *Gerry Blaikie (www.scotcities.com)*

and sewage works. It is not known for certain whether or not he had a particular interest in football although, as he had been born in Glasgow, it is perhaps reasonable to assume that he had, but at all events the idea of designing football stadiums obviously appealed to him – and he decided to embark upon this new branch of his career in his home city.

watch the Varsity men row by. It must have been the only ground in Britain where, once every year or so, almost half the fans turned their backs on the game for a full five minutes. Mind you, they were watching Fulham!

The Stevenage Road Stand cost Fulham £15,000 and, together with its red brick façade (now listed), it is there to this day. The club however also paid for a rather more distinctive feature – a house at one corner of the ground. The original Craven Cottage was long gone, but Leitch was commissioned to build a new one to accommodate offices, a boardroom, a dressing room and, somewhat strangely, a small flat for a player to occupy. Craven Cottage looks in fact like a substantial detached house, and given its location in over-priced southwest London it would probably sell for the best part of £1 million, should it ever be converted and offered for sale as a domestic residence.

Around the period when he was working on the homes of Fulham and Chelsea, Leitch was also designing a stand at Blackburn Rovers' Ewood Park. The main Nuttall Street Stand

Above: **The imposing Stevenage Road façade at Craven Cottage is listed by English Heritage.** *Northdown*

Above right: **Aerial view of Fulham's Craven Cottage before recent rebuilding, with the Stevenage Road Stand nearest the camera and the Cottage in the corner.** *Northdown*

Right: **This view of Everton's Goodison Park during the third round FA Cup tie against King's Lynn in 1962 shows the typical Leitch patterning on the stand.** *Northdown*

cost an impressive £24,000, and its red-bricked frontage was an almost exact replica of that at Craven Cottage. It also featured a fine oak-panelled boardroom. The engineer-cum-architect now had the bit well and truly between his teeth, and within a few years the Archibald Leitch building programme was really under way, with developments at White Hart Lane, Goodison Park and Leeds Road.

At Tottenham's White Hart Lane, Leitch was responsible for the building of the West Stand.

Conference in 1996, 1997 and 1998, by which time Moss Rose had scraped over the qualifying hurdle.

April Fools

When Maidstone United folded in 1992 (having received no help from their fellow clubs and the FA), the League's entry criteria were tightened so that fewer clubs could get in, although they had to be relaxed slightly after Stevenage threatened to take the League to court in 1996. Even now, however, clubs have to have everything in place by (appropriately) 1 April to qualify for promotion in August. By an amazing coincidence, those former League clubs who *have* won the Conference have had no trouble whatsoever in getting back into the League – in spite of the fact that their grounds were in far worse shape than many newcomers.

Margate Nightmare

The then Southern League club Margate were told in 2001 that they needed to upgrade their ageing Hartsdown Park ground if they were to win the championship and seek promotion to the Conference. This would have required the Main Stand to be completely refitted with 500 new seats and a new West Stand would be needed along with new terracing, as well as crowd control barriers, construction of new ladies' toilets, a spectators' treatment room, new press facilities and the erection of new perimeter and internal fencing.

This expenditure was unlikely as Thanet Council were on the point of agreeing to fund a completely new stadium. Unfortunately the ground criteria deadline of 1 April was to be before the championship had been won.

Having partially knocked down their ground and moved in with neighbours Dover, they ended up back at Hartsdown, still knocked down, in an attempt to save money, then moved back to Dover – only to find the Conference threatening to fine them £5,000 per match from the beginning of 2004 to the end of the season for non-compliance with the schedule for returning permanently. At length, they chose to return home to Hartsdown, even though this meant voluntary relegation at the end of the 2003–4 season.

Vics Up Sticks

Northwich Victoria were another club forced to move grounds due to changing criteria. When they were threatened with losing their

Exeter's St James' Park combines two stands with a built-up terracing for home fans at the Big Bank end behind the far goal. *Northdown*

Conference status in 2002 due to the Drill Field's inability to comply with new ground grading criteria, the Vics' board sold the ground to property developers. The club was scheduled to move to the new Victoria Stadium in Wincham for the start of the 2004–5 season, groundsharing at neighbours Witton Albion in the meantime. They currently aim to

Above: **Northwich Victoria's ground in 1980. In 2004 they were to return to a new stadium from lodgings with Witton Albion.** *Robert Lilliman*

Below: **Havant & Waterlooville's West Leigh Park, where Portsmouth play reserve games.** *Northdown*

suitable sites, and Fulham ended their groundshare arrangement in May 2004 to return to Craven Cottage with temporary stands offering seats where once there had been terracing. A groundshare with neighbours Chelsea, who were at least in the borough of Hammersmith and Fulham (a sticking point with stayaway fans who wanted to see Fulham in their home borough), was rejected due to a covenant restricting the number of times the ground was to be used (as a consequence, Chelsea's reserves play at Aldershot).

The possibility of Merseyside rivals Liverpool and Everton sharing arose in 2003 when the local council said public funds could be made available to support a new shared stadium which could hold up to 70,000. The issue saw the possibility of more than 100 years of tradition being consigned to history – ironically, Everton had originally played at Anfield and Liverpool had been formed by Anfield's owner when they left for Goodison Park back in 1892.

One hundred and eleven years later, Liverpool were in the process of preparing a planning application to build a stadium in Stanley Park, which separates the two existing grounds, while Everton remained keen to leave Goodison, which holds 40,170 but is difficult to expand due to its location. A bid to build a new 55,000-seater waterfront stadium at King's Dock had been dropped after Everton failed to raise enough cash to fund the £155 million project.

Liverpool Council were in favour of a joint solution. Chief executive David Henshaw said: 'The future success of both clubs – both on

Anfield, 1966. The ground has been largely rebuilt since then but Liverpool are still keen to relocate to a new stadium.
Ken Coton

and off the field – is critical to the future success of the whole city. It is important that all the options are carefully and thoroughly examined. That must include the groundsharing option.' It should be remembered that Goodison Park was once a state-of-the-art stadium that was chosen ahead of Anfield to host matches in the 1966 World Cup Finals. Two decades after that there was talk of a groundshare, then at Aintree, which never came to anything.

'It's taken 20 years to get round to talking,' said former Red Alan Kennedy, 'but I think it's a particularly good thing and it would be a good idea to have a stadium that is central for everyone.' Presumably this would operate like the San Siro in Milan, where even the souvenir shop is divided down the middle into blue and red sides.

Liverpool's original plan was to swap Anfield for the Stanley Park land, on which they would build the new ground, with the current site of Anfield becoming part of the park. That was deemed unacceptable by English Heritage and CABE (the Commission for Architecture and the Built Environment) who wanted to see some development in the park, rather than 'more windswept open space'. A series of ideas was then developed in conjunction with local people to create a joint venture between club, city and community that might include cafés/restaurants, offices, high-quality open space and an open-air market.

Above: **Newport's Somerton Park ground played host to speedway as well as football.** *Northdown*

Right: **This aerial view of Goodison Park graphically shows the density of surrounding housing and why Everton want to move.** *EFC*

'The concept of the joint venture is to make sure that this new development and, in particular, the park and the cemetery, is always properly maintained, cared for and kept in top quality condition,' said Liverpool chief executive Rick Parry, who pointed out that the development's opening could coincide with the city's selection as European Capital of Culture in 2008, as long as the new stadium opened in 2006.

Rugby clubs have been frequent lodgers at football grounds, most notably at a time when Rugby League was seeking to gain a foothold in the south (via Fulham's team of the 1980s which became the London Broncos) and more recently in Rugby Union with the Zurich Premiership requiring more advanced facilities than most rugby clubs could afford, hence London Irish playing at the Madejski, Wasps buzzing between Loftus Road and Adams Park, Wycombe, and Rotherham playing at Millmoor in 2003–4, having the previous session been denied entry into the elite. Rugby's damage to the playing surface had to be weighed against the financial benefit to the football clubs involved.

A slightly different story was seen in Bradford when, after the fire at Valley Parade, Bradford City lodged temporarily at the Odsal Rugby League Stadium while their home was repaired following the 1985 conflagration. Speedway teams were regular sharers with football at one time, the summer season dovetailing well with the winter game. Newport County's Somerton Park was one of the last of these, replacing greyhound racing there between 1964 and 1977, but a declining market for speedway combined with the impracticality of a cinder

track separating the pitch from spectators has all but ended this. (Interestingly, Newport's speedway promoters switched their attention to Eastville, then the home of Bristol Rovers, just across the Severn Bridge.)

The most audacious groundshare proposal of all came when Arsenal's move to Ashburton Grove appeared likely to founder at the same time as neighbours Tottenham announced their desire to leave White Hart Lane. Given that Wembley had been used for Arsenal's home Champions League games in 1998–9, it seemed possible that the two north London clubs could co-exist in a superb stadium not far from their traditional homes – though Arsenal's poor home record in the Champions League that season made it a non-runner in some supporters' eyes. (Ashburton Grove's funding was finally confirmed in February 2004.)

Arsène Wenger has suggested that clubs having their own grounds is a facet of English football culture

Arsenal stated in written evidence to the Culture, Sport and Tourism Committee of the London Assembly that, if costs continued to rise, permanent groundsharing in the future could not be ruled out. However, they felt it would be a major step which would only work if any shared ground was purpose-built on 'neutral territory'. Manager Arsène Wenger has suggested that clubs having their own grounds is a facet of English football culture.

Milan, Turin and Rome all boast communal stadiums used by more than one club. Yet Turin's Stadio delle Alpi, built for the 1990 World Cup, is unpopular with fans of both Torino and Juventus for its poor atmosphere and both clubs are hoping to return to their former homes. Maybe Merseyside and London fans' natural reluctance isn't so surprising after all.

Tickets and Ticketing

When football first became a popular spectator sport, admission prices were low. In those far off days you could see your team perform for just a few pence, but of course it has to be remembered that wages were also very low. Real comparisons are difficult to make, due to rising standards of living and the increased amount of disposable income available to most during the 20th and early 21st centuries, but it is interesting to note just what sort of money people were earning a hundred or so years ago.

There was little inflation in the early years of the 20th century and wages barely changed from year to year. Shortly before World War 1, a farm worker could expect to earn less than £1 a week, while general labourers in towns earned, on average, about one pound four shillings (£1.20). Miners and skilled engineers did a little better, miners earning about one pound twelve shillings (£1.60), engineers more than £2. Clergymen, with take home pay of around £4, and barristers, who normally made well over £25 a week, did a great deal better. However, it seems unlikely that many clergymen or barristers spent their Saturday afternoons at football matches.

World War 1 saw a period of relatively high inflation and after the conflict those who were able to get a job were likely to be earning a

little more. Prices in general naturally rose accordingly, but football was now the spectator sport of the masses, and it was still very cheap. During the 1930s a place on the terraces would cost a shilling (5p) or perhaps a little bit more. After World War 2 football became more popular than ever and admission prices did begin to rise a little, but they were still very low by the standards of today. For the opening day of the first postwar season in 1946, the Chancellor of the Exchequer decreed that the price of a place on the terraces should not exceed one shilling and threepence (approx 6p) but some clubs did in fact charge an extra threepence for admission to certain parts of the ground.

Immediately after the war, Newcastle United charged half a crown (12.5p) or three shillings and sixpence (17.5p) for a seat, and one shilling and sixpence (7.5p) for a place on the

Left: **Torquay's Plainmoor ground welcomes visitors, 1987.** *Graham Betts*

Top: **Championed by their chairman David Evans, Luton pioneered the membership scheme favoured by Margaret Thatcher, then Prime Minister, in the late 1980s as an answer to football hooliganism. The scheme proved unsuccessful.** *Graham Betts*

vast terraces. Boys (no mention of girls!) and 'Forces' were charged just ninepence (4p). Even by 1953, you could watch Queens Park Rangers play at Loftus Road in the League Division Three (South) for as little as one shilling and ninepence (9p) or, if you could afford to splash out, you could go into the covered enclosure for half a crown (12.5p) or even the stand, for either four shillings and sixpence (22.5p) or six shillings (30p). At this time, the average labourer's wages were in the region of £7 a week. A year earlier, Second Division Fulham were offering season tickets to their Craven Cottage ground for £5 5s, or £8 8s. Interestingly, although they were not mentioned in Fulham's programme advertisement, these prices were actually in guineas – one guinea being equal to one pound and one shilling. The season tickets were for the stand in Stevenage Road, so you could sit and watch the Cottagers' 22 games for an average price of either four shillings 10 pence (24p) or seven shillings seven pence (38p) per game.

Unusually for Conference grounds, Chester's Deva Stadium segregated home and away fans. *Northdown*

Entry to First Division games was generally a little more expensive, but not a lot, and prices rose little over the next few seasons. If you wanted to see Tottenham play Benfica in the European Champions Cup in April 1962, you could stand on the terraces for five shillings (25p) and when England played Spain at Wembley Stadium in May 1967, prices ranged from seven shillings and sixpence (37.5p) for a place on the terraces, to £2 10s (£2.50p) for the best seats. For the 1970 FA Cup semi-final between Chelsea and Watford, played at White Hart Lane, seats cost between £1 and £2 10s (£2.50), while a place on the terraces was to be had for 10 shillings (50p).

Inflation really took off in the mid-1970s, and remained quite high until the late 1980s, and naturally this was reflected in the prices paid to attend football matches.

In 1982 Fulham had just been promoted to the old Second Division and were due to play the likes of Leeds United, Blackburn Rovers, Newcastle and Chelsea. The highest seat price at Craven Cottage was now £4, with terrace

Tottenham Hotspur v Benfica at White Hart Lane ticket. Admittance to a top European match in 1962 cost the princely sum of five shillings (25 pence). *Alan Barrett*

FULHAM FOOTBALL CLUB

Ticket Office: 959-961 Fulham Road London SW6 5HY

BARCLAYCARD PREMIERSHIP

FULHAM v BOLTON WANDERERS

Sat 06 Dec, 2003   Kick Off 3:00 pm

LOFTUS ROAD UPPER STAND

Block NU   Row N   Seat 183   Price: 25.00

Enter via Turnstile Block 8

S25587 Master J Heatley

00273832

RETAIN THIS PORTION OF YOUR TICKET

Above: **A typical computer-generated ticket of the current century includes the purchaser's identity in case of touting.** *Author's collection*

Right: **Non-League tickets rarely specify match, seat or even season.** *Author's collection*

prices set at £2.50 (boys and OAPs £1 – still no mention of girls!). Four years later, after the Cottagers had sunk back to Division Three, their dearest seats were priced at £6, while it now cost £3 to stand on the terraces.

There was, as ever, something of a north/south divide. In 1976, seats at Manchester United's Old Trafford cost from as little as 90p to £1.60. Three years later, prices ranged from £2.10 to £2.70, with a place on the terraces available for £1.20 or £1.40.

An advertisement in a Barnsley programme in 1983 offered seats at Maine Road for Barnsley's game against newly relegated Manchester City for as much as £5. It would however cost Tykes supporters only £1.50 to stand on the terraces. But times would soon be changing.

FARNBOROUGH TOWN F.C.

SEASON 2003 / 2004

ADULT TERRACE

TO BE RETAINED

CALL: **BORO CLUBCALL**

FOR UP-TO-THE-MINUTE NEWS ON THE BORO

09068 44 00 88

Updated regularly with news, interviews and match reports. Calls charged at 60p per minute.

FOR **BORO** SPONSORSHIP DETAILS CALL THE CLUB.

01252 541469

MAIN CLUB SPONSOR: ALEXANDER FRANCIS

708

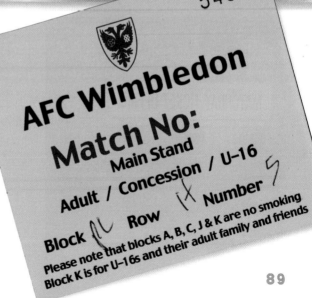

5493

AFC Wimbledon

Match No:

Main Stand

Adult / Concession / U-16

Block ____   Row ____   Number 5

Please note that blocks A, B, C, J & K are no smoking
Block K is for U-16s and their adult family and friends

89

Southampton
HOME SUPPORTERS ONLY
19/08/03

SOUTHAMPTON FOOTBALL CLUB

Merchant No: 4700944
Please Debit my account as detailed ..
Terminal ID: QPADEV0028   Receipt No: 309851
Auth Code: 4960   Transaction No: QPAD309851
Payment Ref: KEYED   Transaction Type: PURCHASE

Switch
Card Nbr: 6759********2656
Expiry Date: 12/04
Card Issue No:

The Saints
Concession   Adult

racism just ain't Saintly

AMOUNT: £   12.00   CUSTOMER NOT PRESENT

SIGNATURE . . . .
. . . .

Thank You
Please Keep Copy

NO SMOKING OR STANDING
IN SEATING AREA

www.saintsfc.co.uk

FRIENDS PROVIDENT

Please use Public Transport for all or part of your journey.

Only valid on the date above or re-arranged date and if detached in the presence of bus driver.

Only valid on the date above or re-arranged date and if detached in the presence of bus driver.

Parking is severely restricted around the stadium.

To be given up   To be given up

Modern Times

In 2003, the average earnings for someone in full-time employment were in the region of £25,000 a year – close to £500 a week – although this figure masks a wide variation across the country, and of course much depends on what you actually do for a living (most writers earn considerably less!). The rise in earnings does however mean that more and more people are able to afford the inflated prices charged by Premier and Football League clubs. Had executive boxes been available before World War 1, they would doubtless have been filled by those wealthy clergymen and barristers, but hardly anyone else would have been able to afford them. Today, corporate entertainment means that people from all walks of life are sometimes able to enjoy the

Southampton's computer-generated ticketing features a picture of their St Mary's Stadium. *Author's collection*

prawn sarnies and champagne, but most supporters are content with a seat in a nice new sponsored stand or, if there are any, a place on the terraces.

Advances in technology have meant that one can now obtain match tickets via computerised systems. Tickets can be ordered using credit and debit cards and, in some cases, via the Internet. Many major clubs now offer external ticket agencies blocks of seats, to be sold telephonically or via the Internet. This may mean transaction/handling charges and postage being added to face value, all of which can elevate the price of a ticket quite considerably. On the plus side, the days of queuing round the block for high-profile games seem to have disappeared.

All this modernisation does of course have to be paid for, but the principal reason for the massive increase in the cost of watching football has been the dramatic rise in players' wages and the spiralling cost of transfers. There is evidence to suggest that both wages and transfer fees may now have peaked, with some clubs capping wages and many relying increasingly on the loan system, rather than paying ludicrous fees for players who are sometimes not much better than ordinary. But

MATCHDAY TICKET OFFICE

The antiquated but charming ticket office at Fulham's Craven Cottage ground. *Northdown*

Pompey Crimes?

When Portsmouth published their prices for the February 2004 FA Cup fifth round tie against Liverpool there was an outcry. Adult tickets at between £28 and £35, pensioners at £26 and £23 for juniors – surely a case of profiteering?

Not so! With three sides of their Fratton Park ground (capacity 19,179) occupied by season-ticket holders, the only area of the ground available on a match-by-match basis was a small section of the uncovered Milton End not occupied by away fans. The prices quoted were for a Category A game – which Pompey's 1-0 win undoubtedly was.

With Portsmouth in the First Division, a family of four in the lower North Stand would have had to pay £50: £16 per adult and £9 per child. In the Premiership, were individual tickets available there, it would be £33 adults and £22 children, the £110 total being a 120% increase. That is the most extreme example, overall prices in the ground having risen 'just' 73%.

Clearly, although newly arrived Premiership clubs receive a £15 million windfall from Sky television, the increased level of player salaries, signing on fees, transfer fees and agents' fees demand prices be hiked. In Portsmouth's case, however, having the second smallest ground in the 2003–4 Premiership plus a total lack of executive boxes put the squeeze on even a multi-millionaire like chairman Milan Mandaric. And the situation, by no means out of the ordinary, shows just how out of touch the game has become in financial terms with the man and woman in the street.

The Milton End, the only uncovered portion of Portsmouth's Fratton Park. *M. Heatley*

it still costs a good few million to sign a top-flight striker.

Time was when the best British players often looked to the Continent in order to increase their earning capacity. Now it tends to be the other way round, with European and other foreign players coming to this country to seek, or perhaps to further, their fortunes. These players have helped make the Premiership one of the most competitive leagues in the world, but there has been a price to pay, and it is the supporter who, one way or another, pays it.

Market Forces

For Scottish Premier League games, the average seat normally costs about £16 – unless the home side is playing Rangers or Celtic, in which case the price will probably rise to something in the region of £20 to £25 – prices similar to those charged by the big two for their home games. By contrast, you can watch Third Division Montrose for £7 (standing) or £7.50 (seated).

In England, too, Premiership clubs usually categorise games so that, for example, Tottenham Hotspur may charge their own fans anything from £25 to £55 per game (depending also upon the location of the seat) and Chelsea (probably the most expensive club to visit) anything from £31 to £67. Prices in the lower divisions are naturally somewhat lower, and they tend to be lower too in the

The Cup That Cheers

Cup runs have often supplied the wherewithal for clubs to improve their grounds, and this is a tradition that continues to this day. Unlike League games, where the home side pockets the gate receipts, monies from FA and League Cup ties are still split 45%–45% between the opposing teams, the governing body taking the remaining 10%.

In 1955 York City narrowly missed out on a visit to Wembley in the FA Cup Final, losing to Newcastle United in a semi-final replay. The profit made that season was spent on an extension to the Main Stand. When Bootham Crescent was fitted with floodlights (costing £14,500) in 1959, the first game they were used for was, appropriately, a friendly against Newcastle on 28 October.

York's 1985 FA Cup run included games against Arsenal (beaten 1-0 at home) and Liverpool, the latter going to a replay (lost 7-0) in front of an Anfield crowd of 43,000. Improvements which this funded included building hospitality suites behind the Main Stand, new club offices, turnstiles, crush barriers and more seats added to the Popular Stand, making the number of seats 2,883 out of a total capacity of 13,185.

In 2004, Kidderminster Harriers' third round FA Cup tie with neighbours Wolverhampton Wanderers attracted a record 6,005 paying spectators to the Aggborough Stadium. (Some way short of the 9,155 that saw them play Hereford in 1948 but twice the 2002–3 average of 2,895.) When their 1-0 lead was pegged back in the penultimate minute, chairman Colin Youngjohns was still smiling. 'To have won would have been unbelievable,' he said. 'We have taken on the Wolves first team and almost beat them. But even if we'd got through we couldn't have hoped for better than Wolves away, so we win all the way down the line.' An estimated £100,000 raised by the replay would, Youngjohns said, pay for renovations to the Main Stand as well as covering recent improvements to the floodlights. Little wonder relative newcomers Kidderminster were one of only around half a dozen clubs in the Football League to record an annual profit – with a little help from lady luck.

north of England. In the 2003–4 season Carlisle United, relegated from the Third Division at the end of the campaign, charged £11 for a place on the terraces, and £14 for a seat in the stands, while Premiership side Manchester City charged from £18 (in the Family Stand) to £32 for 90 minutes' football in their new stadium. Their dearly beloved neighbours, Manchester United, currently charge between £25 and £29 for a seat – if you can get one. If you can't, you can always stand outside and read their £3 programme instead. Of course, you could transfer your affections to a team playing in the lower reaches of the Football League, where additional income may be desperately needed in order to stave off a visit from the Official Receiver.

The purchase of a season ticket can reduce the overall outlay, but even so, few Premiership clubs offer them for less than £450 and some charge considerably more.

Football has for some time been big business and clubs need to raise revenue wherever they can. In the Premiership and, to a much lesser extent, in the coca-Cola League, 'television money' has assumed increasing importance. But clubs also raise money by other means, and in recent years evenings of entertainment have become increasingly popular. In October 2003, you could enjoy such an evening at Stamford Bridge with Surrey and England's cricketing hero Alec Stewart. This cost £40, which, for Chelsea, seems quite reasonable, especially as a three-course meal was included. Many clubs bring back elderly ex-players from time to time, especially if they are able to make a passable after-dinner speech, and it all helps to raise revenue.

But still it is the ordinary supporter who has to shell out. A day out for the family at Old Trafford is likely to cost well in excess

Exeter's double-glazed doors honour their sponsor. *Northdown*

of £100 (even more if the family regularly travels up from southeast England!) and costs can only increase as time goes by. In 1897 you could buy a dozen football shirts for your team for little more than £1. The same amount today might, if you're lucky, just buy you a swift half at your club's bar.

This is what visiting supporters might have expected to pay at English Premiership grounds in season 2003-4:		
	Adult (£)	Concession (£)
Arsenal	31.00	15.50
Aston Villa	22.00	12.00 to 16.00
Birmingham City	30.00 to 38.00	15.00 to 19.00
Blackburn Rovers	23.00 to 28.00	5.00 to 18.00
Bolton Wanderers	19.00 to 31.00	9.00 to 22.00
Charlton Athletic	20.00 to 35.00	15.00 to 25.00
Chelsea	31.00 to 49.00	None
Everton	20.50 to 28.00	13.00 to 19.00
Fulham	26.00 to 30.00	12.00 to 21.00
Leeds United	22.00 to 29.00	15.00 to 19.00
Leicester City	22.00 to 32.00	17.00 to 27.00
Liverpool	26.00 to 29.00	13.00 to 14.50
Manchester City	18.00 to 32.00	10.00 to 12.00
Manchester United	25.00 to 29.00	12.50 to 14.50
Middlesbrough	15.00 to 22.00	14.00 to 16.00
Newcastle United	27.00	14.00 to 23.00
Portsmouth	25.00 to 29.00	14.00 to 20.00
Southampton	24.00 to 28.00	11.00 to 23.00
Tottenham Hotspur	25.00 to 40.00	None
Wolverhampton Wanderers	29.00	15.00
Note: some clubs also have a few seats at higher prices.		

Conference football could be watched in 2003–4 for less than a tenner. *M. Heatley*

Advertising and Entertainment

If time is money, the frenetic pace and unprecedented rewards of football in the 21st century make it a more valuable commodity than ever. And with images of Sir Alex Ferguson pacing the touchline, staring pointedly at his watch, it's little surprise that almost every ground in Britain features some form of timepiece.

Few have been as celebrated as that which gave the Clock End at Highbury its popular name. Improvements in 1989 saw 53 VIP lounges installed in the South Stand (its other name), which accommodates away fans, as does a portion of the West Stand.

These days, the time is usually displayed digitally, as at Loftus Road where a dot-matrix indicator at the School End combines time with latest score. Few grounds will now let their clocks 'tick' beyond 45 minutes for fear of the true amount of injury/added time indicated being held against the referee should his calculations not coincide.

Half-time scoreboards appear, by and large,

to be a thing of the past. It was customary for programmes to list the day's other fixtures with a letter added: numbered plates would then be appended to the letters which were displayed – eg A 2:0; B 1:3, etc. Fulham were a club which tried to be different, having an illuminated sign hanging from the roof of the Hammersmith End at Craven Cottage that displayed letters A through to F. According to which colour light was being used at the time, these six 'fixtures' could serve to illustrate 30-36 scores, but in practice this led to confusion among the 95% of fans whose vision was less than 20/20 – and that's not a score!

Public address (PA) systems have long been a bone of contention and remain as important as ever. They allow team changes, goal times and other relevant match information to be imparted and, most importantly, can co-ordinate evacuation should there be an emergency. Unfortunately, in at least 70% of grounds, the PA system is considered inadequate by most fans.

The half-time scores have yet to reach Leeds Road, Huddersfield, in the 1972–3 season. *Ken Coton*

Newcastle's matchday announcer chose the League Cup match against lowly Leyton Orient at St James' Park in September 2000 to take a night off. Fans reported 'sporadic outbursts of white noise emanating from the speakers, which I thought was from a Velvet Underground live bootleg tape'. Others identified this as 'Darth Vader making an obscene phone call', 'the voice of the Mysterons' or 'the ghost of (former chairman) Lord Westwood, rattling the corrugated iron at the back of the old Leazes with his hook'.

Another Tannoy announcer to have a bad night was the man on duty at Anfield in February 2004 when Liverpool entertained Levski Sofia in the UEFA Cup. The *Daily Mail* reported that, plugging a club-produced DVD entitled *The Great Managers*, he managed to rechristen the legendary Bob Paisley 'Bill'. Then, as the visitors made a second-half substitute, he revealed his uncertainty by announcing that 'Number 25, Whatdoesthatsay' had entered the field of play!

Some clubs use personalities as pre-match masters of ceremonies. Fulham's David Hamilton, now a broadcaster on Heart FM, is well known for his days on Radio 1, while Leicester's Alan Birchenall is a former player whose prowess with a radio microphone has become almost as legendary as his goalscoring skills.

DJ David Hamilton, Fulham's matchday master of ceremonies. *Northdown*

Sheffield United recognised the importance of the PA and in 2000 instituted a two-phase plan to provide spectators with what it called an 'an entertainment spectacular', aiming to encourage fans into the stadium as early as possible. The club required its new system to provide an intelligible sound for over 20,000

'Good quality sound equipment ensures an electric crowd atmosphere that cannot be appreciated at home'

people – something the existing 2,000-watt system had not proved suitable for. Like so many stadiums of its era, Bramall Lane suffered from messy sound reverberation. A number of enclosures were distributed across the ground to ensure that crowds would both enjoy music and hear announcements clearly. The new PA system boasted an output capability of 18,000 watts (RMS), while the original PA system was retained for the exclusive use of the emergency services.

After installation the club experienced increased ticket sales, an electric atmosphere and positive spectator involvement on matchdays. John Thurman, managing director of Sheffield United, said: 'Good quality sound equipment ensures an electric crowd atmosphere that cannot be appreciated at home. It was frustrating to listen to an announcement, let alone music of any type, over the old PA system; it just seemed to garble and create echoes. This new system has made a world of difference [and] spectator involvement has increased ten-fold. It even seems to have given our team a competitive edge on our home ground, which is reflected in our recent at-home results.'

Phase two of the installation project involved a large LED screen to provide the audience with synchronised vision and sound. Many grounds now have such big screens, or 'Jumbotrons' as they are known, on which match action can be replayed. The newly redeveloped White Hart Lane has a Jumbotron video screen built into the roof at each end of this ground, while Selhurst Park was unusual among non-top-flight grounds before Palace's recent promotion, in having big-screen capability. One-time tenants Wimbledon, however, were allowed to use it only as a scoreboard – ironically the one thing Palace seem not to use it for – as they failed to contribute to the £1 million cost of the screens and surround-sound PA system (wags suggested their crowds would have been satisfied with 'a 14-inch TV set from Dixons at the front of the Holmesdale').

Arsenal's two jumbo screens offer pre-match, half-time, and post-match entertainment, which includes highlights of previous games and interviews. It also assists in the pre-match entertainment, which has moved on from brass bands to feature dancers, cheerleaders, mascot races and even tribute bands. This ritual has become increasingly important in economic terms in getting supporters into the ground early and spending money while there.

Perhaps the Jumbotron's biggest claim to fame came in its use at a Canadian gridiron game where Pamela Anderson was selected from the spectators for a close-up. In Britain, however, the screens are used to show team

Half-time entertainment of the old school.
Ken Coton

Pre-match Entertainment

The military brass bands that used to do untold pre-match damage to the playing surface have now been replaced by the lighter tread of dance troupes such as West Ham's Hammerettes and Fulham's Cravenettes. (Both coming from the same stable, it's rumoured the same dancers do double duty as the clubs play at home on alternate Saturdays.) Remarkably, to celebrate Fulham's return to Craven Cottage in August 2004, The Cravenettes were replaced by a troupe of male dancers who were introduced as 'The Gayvanettes'.

Club mascots are often employed to wander the pitch dispensing sweets and souvenirs to younger supporters – Everton's Toffee Girl is perhaps the longest-established of these – while bands and tribute acts have also been tried. The secret is to get crowds to the ground early, thus reducing the strain on the turnstile area and, just as importantly, giving supporters more time to spend their money.

Above: **Crystal Palace's team of cheerleaders, the Crystals, are every bit as well-drilled as Iain Dowie's first XI.** *Jean Eve*

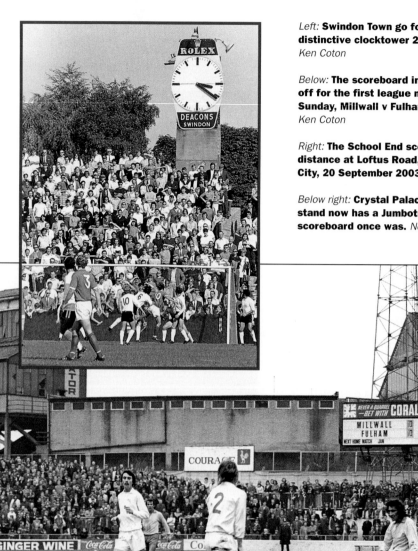

Left: **Swindon Town go for goal in front of their distinctive clocktower 21 minutes into a match.** *Ken Coton*

Below: **The scoreboard indicates an early kick-off for the first league match played on a Sunday, Millwall v Fulham, 20 January 1974.** *Ken Coton*

Right: **The School End scoreboard glows in the distance at Loftus Road, Fulham v Manchester City, 20 September 2003.** *Northdown*

Below right: **Crystal Palace's Holmesdale End stand now has a Jumbotron screen where this scoreboard once was.** *Northdown*

The Jumbotron screen at Highbury's Clock End shows pre-match highlights. *Northdown*

line-ups, plus replays of goal action. It's rare for contentious incidents to be replayed, however, as this has brought warnings from the FA against encouraging crowd trouble.

These screens can be used to project advertisements before the match and at half-time. Also visually stimulating, although on a smaller scale, is the new style of pitch-side advertising hoarding which 'flips' from one ad to another as play continues. These are particularly effective and eye-catching for television viewers, and increase the amount of revenue that may be obtained by the club. These rolling, constantly changing electronic hoardings were already in regular use in France, Spain and the US when Britons saw them for the first time on the Channel 5 broadcast of England's World Cup game in Albania in March 2001. The TV station's switchboard was swamped with viewers complaining about them.

It was suggested the FA look into the possibility that players might be distracted by them, but Skyville, the British agency selling the advertising space, insisted that the LED digital boards were tilted upwards at such an angle that the players could not possibly be affected. This form of advertising is clearly here to stay, and will doubtless be incorporated into stadiums of the future.

Pardeep Saran, a senior partner at UK

Southampton's St Mary's Stadium boasts a Jumbotron screen at either end of the pitch. *M. Heatley*

marketing agency Skyville, believes the growth of LED perimeter advertising in the UK, when compared to its popularity in Spain, for example, has been held back by the nature of our stadiums. 'UK grounds are technically the smallest in Europe and on the Continent advertising hoardings are typically 1m high, which is the height utilised by manufacturer ISO (International Sports Organisation) for LED technology. In the UK they are 0.6m high. While there is interest from many English Premier League clubs in LED advertising, they face having to remove perhaps the first three rows of seating in order to accommodate the higher screens that are required.'

Skyville had investigated using another supplier that could provide screens with 0.6m specifications but found that they collapsed when a ball hit them. LED technology also works better during evening matches than daylight ones – a problem when so many UK soccer matches kick off around 3pm, compared to the number of evening fixtures in Spain.

A more old-fashioned but also novel take on advertising comes in the shape of stand roofs intended to catch the eye of those flying overhead. Brentford's Griffin Park, on the flight path to London's busy Heathrow Airport, has long sported such slogans, while Fulham followed suit further along the Thames.

Perhaps the ultimate roof-mounted advertising gimmick, however, was recently to be seen on the South Stand of Aldershot's Recreation Ground. The roof overhung the seats, with an advert for Unibond adhesive across the front. This was strangely eye-catching when viewed from the other side of the pitch, as the advert demonstrated the glue's stickability by having a washing machine stuck to the front of the roof of the stand! Home supporters are still waiting for the day the washing machine slides off – and no jokes about clean sheets!

Above: **Once an expanse of terracing, the seated North Stand at Fratton Park reflects the club sponsor's identity.** *M. Heatley*

Below: **Chester City's novel answer to declining crowds – an advert on wheels.** *Northdown*

MER SPORTS GOODS
DON ROAD ● PHONE 23694

Above: **While most grounds had pitch-side ads, the Archers Road end at Southampton's late, lamented Dell in 1966 was different.** *Ken Coton*

Left: **With attendances of around 1,000, sponsorship deals are crucial to the survival of Conference clubs like Tamworth and Forest Green.** *M. Heatley*

Right: **Football's family values are now attractive to advertisers, as this sponsored stand at Witton shows.** *M. Heatley*

Advertising hoardings on the riverbank as Fulham's George Cohen goes forward. *Ken Coton*

Brentford's 1992 sponsors advertise themselves in more ways than one. *Lee Doyle*

Behind the Scenes

If dressing rooms could talk, what stories they could tell. How about Old Trafford's hallowed home dressing room where, in February 2003 after a match with arch-rivals Arsenal which saw United dumped out of the FA Cup, Sir Alex Ferguson left fly with the boot that not only damaged David Beckham but also, it seems, put in train his transfer to Real Madrid? 'It's just one of those things,' said a clearly embarrassed Becks of the very visible cut. 'It's all in the past now.' But who believed him?

Teacups have flown in many a dressing room over the years, at half and full time – but only once have the facilities been blamed for a manager getting the sack. That's what happened in August 2003 when West Ham visited Rotherham's Millmoor ground. It's not unusual for players to have to change in prefabricated buildings – even West Ham and

opponents did this when the Bobby Moore Stand was being built – but Glenn Roeder was reportedly persuaded to let his players return to their hotel to change, there not being room for the whole squad. The Hammers' subsequent defeat and accusations of their being 'southern softies' may well have contributed to his removal from office shortly afterwards.

The referee's room is normally out of bounds to players and managers alike, save for the handing over of the team sheets before kick-off. Robbie Savage found himself in more than hot water while playing for Leicester City at Filbert Street against Villa in April 2002. Finding himself caught short during the warm-up, he

Shirts hang ready in the Withdean dressing room for Brighton's promotion-winning Division 2 side, 2003–4. *BHAFC*

Left: **Fulham chairman Tommy Trinder inspects the dressing room at Blackpool's Bloomfield Road ground.** *Ken Coton*

Below left: **The Craven Cottage home dressing room in the 1970s. It would still look familiar to players three decades later.** *Ken Coton*

On the Coach

When Bolton visited Tranmere Rovers in August 2000, manager Sam Allardyce instructed his players to board the team coach immediately after their 1-0 victory and travel back to their own Reebok Stadium to shower and change rather than use the Prenton Park facilities. It is believed, however, that this stemmed from his feud with Tranmere manager John Aldridge rather than disdain for the Birkenhead team's ground. There had been some sharp exchanges between the managers in games during the previous season which included two legs of the League Cup semi-final which Tranmere won 4-0 on aggregate.

Right: **Chelsea's physio administers treatment to an injured player at Stamford Bridge, 1970s.** *Ken Coton*

Below: **Republic of Ireland international Jimmy Conway on the Craven Cottage treatment table in the early 1970s.** *Ken Coton*

When it comes to provision of dugouts, even a multi-million pound club like Chelsea (below) can be put in the shade by Witton (above), whose sponsors happen to be double-glazing specialists! *D. Heatley*

The Long Walk

Dugouts are customarily on the same side of the ground from which the players emerge: Bristol Rovers' Memorial Stadium, Hartlepool's Victoria Ground and Fulham's Craven Cottage are three exceptions which require the management and substitutes to cross the playing area. This can cause problems when players are asked to take an early bath; their progress around the perimeter of the pitch will often be accompanied by spectator comment from the closest of quarters.

disappeared into referee Graham Poll's room to relieve himself, thereby kicking off what became known as the 'Jobbiegate' scandal.

'Much has been said and written about what happened that day,' said Savage, 'but I was on two lots of antibiotics at the time for a kick on my leg, which resulted in an upset stomach. I had a bad case of diarrhoea on the day of the game, so had to go there and then, and the nearest place was the referee's toilet. Most people in my situation wouldn't have played that day, but I wanted to help Leicester get out of their predicament and the tablets issued came from the club.

> 'I had a bad case of diarrhoea on the day of the game, so had to go there and then, and the nearest place was the referee's toilet'

'There is no way in the world I would use the referee's toilet deliberately, but if I found myself in an identical situation, I would do exactly the same thing. The fact that I could still get banned for three games would, I feel, be a real injustice, so I'll be arguing my case fervently and hope the FA will see my point of view on this one.' He eventually decided not to appeal against the £10,000 fine – surely the costliest penny spent by a professional player in the history of the game.

The communal plunge bath was always the norm in the days when showers were considered effete. Malcolm Allison made better use of the photo opportunity than most when inviting 'Penthouse' Pet' Fiona Richmond to share a nude bath with Crystal Palace footballers at Selhurst Park at the end of the 1976 season. The much-photographed communal dip sparked off a row in the soccer world, and Allison was accused of bringing the game into disrepute. The former Manchester City boss parted company with the Third Division club after a season in which they reached the FA Cup semi-final and narrowly missed promotion.

Creature Comforts

Toilets

The provision of refreshments at football matches was beginning to assume a greater importance in the 1960s, but the provision of lavatories was not. Women, it seems, did not exist! It is, of course, true that relatively few female supporters attended football matches up until the 1960s, but those who did needed to have very strong bladders. By the time she had found a 'ladies' at the ground (if she ever did), the average woman would have battled her way through thousands of cloth-capped men in search of relief. By the time she had found her way back to her place on the terraces, she would probably have missed most of the game.

As recently as 1986, a visiting woman supporter at Chester City's old Sealand Road ground found no 'ladies' adjacent to the visitors' terracing, and had to ask a policeman for assistance. The officer duly unlocked a gate and pointed towards a narrow passageway behind the stand. When reached, the toilet turned out to be in total darkness. (Thankfully, this book provides pictorial evidence that the 'gents', at least, is adequately lit in the new Deva Stadium; Sealand Road is now lying under an industrial park!)

Below left: **The gents' at Shrewsbury's Gay Meadow ground, one of the more 'traditional' football venues.** *Northdown*

Below: **A view inside the gents' at Chester's Deva Stadium – new ground, new loos.**

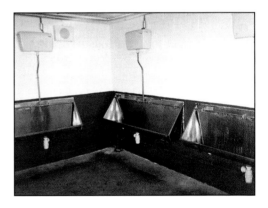

Even Wembley Stadium had little provision for the comfort of women. The FA Cup Final of 1952, between Newcastle and Arsenal, was expected to attract about 5,000 women supporters (5% of the total crowd) but female toilet facilities were extremely limited. In addition, it was suddenly realised that, following the death of King George VI in February, the new Queen would be in attendance at the Final in May. A special toilet therefore had to be constructed near to the royal box. It is not known whether or not Her Majesty used the special royal facilities, but given that she is unlikely to have drunk several pints of Watney's

Witton's Wincham Park was built in 1989 with a toilet block. *M. Heatley*

before the game, it is more than possible that the royal loo remained unvisited.

At grounds throughout the country, the standard facilities for 'gentlemen' comprised a double-entrance/exit arrangement housing a long trough – not so very different from today, except that these outbuildings were often open to the sky, and stainless steel urinals with automatic flushing facilities were as yet unheard of. Cubicles, where a gentleman could sit and read the programme at half-time, were seldom available to those who occupied the terraces.

As they had, unlike the Queen, often downed a pint or three before the game, gentleman supporters were likely to need the facilities on several occasions during the course of an afternoon. It was not too bad if you happened to be standing somewhere near the back but if you were in the middle of the terracing, you had a problem. Rolled-up newspapers were known to have been employed, but if you could hold out until half-time you could join the surge

towards the official facilities. The difficulty was that, as well as being of a very basic nature, the urinals were of insufficient size to accommodate large numbers of men with bursting bladders. Inevitably, some people simply went up against the wall.

Cubicles, where a gentleman could sit and read the programme at half-time, were seldom available to those who occupied the terraces.

When Fulham took up residence at Loftus Road for a two-year term, chairman Mohamed Al Fayed found himself missing the creature comforts afforded him at Craven Cottage where, legend has it, the glass in his executive box in the Riverside Stand was bullet-proofed. He had a special lavatory installed for himself in the South Africa Road Stand at a rumoured cost of £10,000, though, having fallen out with the British authorities and taken off to Switzerland, his opportunities to christen the installation became fewer and further between.

As those entitled to inspect this custom-built convenience are equally rare, the rumour that the WC contains gold-plated fittings and seat has not been confirmed. One man who does know but is keeping it to himself is BBC Radio Five Live's Mark Clemmit, who, while travelling about 28,000 miles in 2003–4 to visit every League club in the country, not only interviewed Al Fayed but also became the first person, other than the Fulham chairman himself, to use his personal toilet. Apparently, when he went to Wrexham, Clemmit shared the Racecourse Ground stalls with Sir Alex Ferguson, who was there to watch his son Darren, so maybe he is an expert on such matters.

Lavatories in football stadiums have, along with most other things, been seriously upgraded in recent years. Many smaller grounds still have the odd gentlemen's trough which is open to the elements, but the larger grounds mainly have modern, integrated facilities for both men and women – some even providing soft toilet paper. These improvements are more than welcome, although queues are still liable to form at peak periods.

The thorny problem of toilets for the disabled is covered elsewhere.

Executive Boxes

As football's profile has changed, so clubs have attempted to 'upgrade the matchday experience'. The first stage was to create a Vice Presidents' Bar where those who had paid the appropriate annual fee could enjoy pre-match and half-time refreshments without queuing with the common man.

The standard of facilities demanded by and available to supporters has increased markedly in the past two decades. *Ken Coton*

This quickly developed into the executive box, hireable on a season-long or match-by-match basis, where companies can entertain guests and watch the game from behind glass. In theory, at least, it is still impossible to drink alcohol during the match while in view of the pitch – Manchester City-supporting rockers Oasis reportedly had their lager confiscated during one visit to Craven Cottage.

Portsmouth's Fratton Park is currently the only Premier League ground which has no executive boxes. Clubs where demand exceeds supply, such as Chelsea, will use facilities close to the stadium for pre-and post-match entertainment: in this case, the hospitality takes place in the Chelsea Village hotel complex integral with the ground. Former players will often be employed as 'hosts', eg Gordon Davies at Fulham, Peter Osgood at Southampton and Martin Chivers at Tottenham. Prices for one-off games are likely to range from £200 to £300 per person.

Above left: **Fulham's Riverside Stand, built in the 1970s, incorporated executive boxes.** *Ken Coton*

Below: **Filbert Street in the late 1970s catered for corporate customers. Leicester City v Fulham, 22 September 1979.** *Ken Coton*

Car parking is an important creature comfort, and Hull's new KC Stadium (above) is well blessed;
Brechin City's Glebe Park (below) is less so. *Robert Lilliman/Chris Mason*

Examples of Executive Packages on Offer for Season 2003–4

Tottenham Hotspur
White Hart Lane's executive boxes house between 8 and 18 guests:

- Access to box holders' lounge
- Complimentary beers, wines and soft drinks in box
- Four-course luncheon with wines and liqueurs
- Tea and coffee at half-time
- Post-match buffet
- Official programme
- Car parking tickets

Newcastle United
St James' Park's corporate facilities are always in demand:

- Champagne reception
- Complimentary beers, wines and soft drinks
- Four-course meal with wine followed by coffee and mints
- Best seats in West Upper Stand

- Guest celebrity speaker
- Post-match buffet
- Matchday programme
- Corporate gift

Everton
Goodison Park executive boxes have been recently refurbished and can hold 10, 12 or 20 guests:

- Champagne reception
- Private table in the Executive Suite
- Silver Service five-course gourmet set meal with complimentary liqueurs
- Two car park passes per box
- Complimentary drinks served at half-time

The boardroom at Middlesbrough's Riverside Stadium – a sight reserved for those with money and influence. *Ken Coton*

Care in the Football Community

First Aid Facilities

Mention the words 'St John Ambulance' to most people, and their reply is likely to be: 'You mean those people in black and white at football matches?' Formed in 1887, St John Ambulance is the UK's leading provider of first aid care. Its volunteers, all of whom are fully qualified in first aid and many of whom have further medical qualifications, regularly give their time free to provide first aid cover at Premier and Football League games. The clubs pay a nominal fee, but as with all St John's activities the majority of the running costs are covered by donations. Only a small number of senior football clubs use private medical teams: Exeter use 1st Response private ambulance and care services, based in their own city.

The number of first aid personnel required to be on duty reflects the expected attendance, and is laid down in the Taylor Report.

Disabled Fans

Among its many recommendations, the 1990 Taylor Report included provision for disabled fans. The report's author recognised the fact that facilities for the disabled had long been provided on an *ad hoc* basis. Most clubs had space for a few pitch-side wheelchairs, but there was little recognition of other disabilities. A fan with little or no sight would often have to stand on the terraces with everyone else and rely on a friend to tell him or her what was going on.

In June 1998 the Football Task Force published a report on improving the access to facilities for disabled supporters. This proved to be a major step forward as the report stressed the need for swift action. It stated that there should be full consultation with disabled fans for new stadium developments, and there should be annual visits to all 92 League grounds to audit the facilities and

St John Ambulance personnel, a reassuringly familiar sight to all sports lovers, on duty at Oxford's Kassam Stadium. *St John's*

monitor progress. The National Association of Disabled Supporters (NADS) was to be given responsibility for this monitoring.

NADS has published details of facilities at all League, and many non-League, grounds. Although there is still a very long way to go, it's clear that things are changing fast. Unsurprisingly, it is the newly built stadiums which generally offer the best facilities, although a lot of other clubs appear to be doing their best. There are many ongoing initiatives, an example of which is Fulham's bid to raise £35,000 for a fully equipped minibus to take disabled supporters to away games.

NADS gives star ratings to a number of clubs. Wigan Athletic head the list, with 200 spaces for home wheelchair users, 70 seats for the visually impaired (with Hospital Radio commentary via headsets) and a further 70 seats for the hearing impaired at the JJB Stadium. Derby County provide 152 wheelchair places, and again Hospital Radio is available for those wishing to take advantage of it. Derby

also have a ferry service to transport the disabled from the car park to their still relatively new Pride Park stadium.

Middlesbrough have 100 wheelchair places. Those with visual impairment may sit anywhere in the Riverside Stadium, and commentary is provided. Reading's Madejski Stadium also has 100 places for wheelchairs, with a dozen seats available for those who need Hospital Radio commentary, while Sheffield Wednesday have 80 wheelchair places at Hillsborough. All these clubs provide similar facilities for away

'Facilities for disabled football supporters should be an integral part of stadium development, not an optional extra.'

The Taylor Report, 1990

Above: **Unusually, Exeter City employ a privately-run first aid team.** *Northdown*

Right: **Visiting fans at Chesterfield's Saltergate ground smile for the camera.** *Ken Coton*

supporters, although inevitably on a smaller scale. Toilet facilities are also much improved, with some clubs providing dedicated stewards and alarm cord facilities.

Clubs which now have their own disabled supporters' associations include Everton and Manchester United. EDSA (Everton Disabled Supporters' Association) was formed in July 1995. Its main concern is to represent and promote the interests of disabled Evertonians, but it is also concerned with helping other supporters to form their own groups. The association's successes have to date included better access to refreshment areas and full access to the Everton Megastore. MUDSA (Manchester United Disabled Supporters' Association) has its own website. It also produces a magazine, entitled *Rollin' Reds*, organises dinners and other events, and sells its own merchandise including badges and pens.

The Aims and Objectives of NADS (The National Association of Disabled Supporters)

- Carry out an audit of all Premier League, Football League and Conference grounds and facilities.

- Produce and distribute a new national guide to these grounds based on the complete audit programme.

- Offer clubs an impartial advice service on improving existing facilities and planning future developments.

- Offer a structure of support to newly formed supporters' associations (DSA) and assist those working to set up their own DSA.

- Continue to establish itself as the national voice of disabled supporters.

Irvin Morris AWADS

Above: **Wrexham's Racecourse Ground extols the virtues of local ale, 1980.** *Ken Coton*

Right: **The facilities at St James' Park, Exeter, hardly rival their northern counterpart's.** *Northdown*

From the late 1950s, most people were beginning to have more money in their pockets, and although some clubs did not at first cotton on to the fact that they could raise extra revenue by providing refreshments themselves, many soon jumped on the bandwagon. They were not of course able to charge the exorbitant prices that are charged today, but they did their best.

It was during the 1960s that club directors began to talk about football being a business. Perhaps this was because, as self-made businessmen themselves, many of them were duly horrified at the way in which the investment they had made in their beloved football club was being steadily eroded. Costs were continually rising, attendances were drifting downwards

and, in 1961, the maximum wage for players was abolished. Transfer fees were beginning to get out of hand, so the raising of additional revenue assumed greater importance.

For most, it was however still a matter of pies and Bovril. Lifelong Chelsea supporter Alan Barrett recalls his early days at Stamford Bridge:

'As a boy in the 1950s we never bought refreshments, other than some sweets on the way to the match, which we normally saw off long before kick-off. As a young adult supporter in the 1960s, I stood at the Shed end, behind the goal, and part of the matchday ritual was to get Bovril and a pie from the snack bar at the end of the East Stand. We always went there when we arrived at the ground, paying a tanner (2.5p) for the Bovril and about a shilling (5p) for the pie. We then went up to our pitch on the terrace and often stood near to a rather well-spoken Kensington type called Maxwell, who always had a flask of whisky on cold days. He used to pass this around, and often ended up not getting any himself. He never complained and seemed to love the camaraderie, and the fact that he was accepted as one of the lads.

'Last season, I was back at the Bridge with a £40 ticket for the Newcastle match. I had a pre-match drink and a prawn sandwich, and visited the Chelsea Village luxury lavatory, before taking my seat in the East Stand. I suspect Maxwell was sitting comfortably with

Traditional football food is firmly on the menu at most lower division/non-League grounds, such as at Tamworth's Mad-Cor-Als servery.
Northdown

> 'As a young adult supporter in the 1960s, I stood at the Shed end, behind the goal, and part of the matchday ritual was to get Bovril and a pie from the snack bar at the end of the East Stand.'

his hip flask nearby – now surrounded by a better class of supporter.'

The provision of refreshments has been subjected to radical change. Pies, hot dogs and cold tea may still be available but, like everything else, they are no longer inexpensive. To be fair, however, the tea is usually on the hot side of warm, even if it does consist of a single teabag on a piece of string, dumped unceremoniously into a plastic beaker.

Competition in the Kitchen

Football's culinary superstars enjoyed their own cup final in February 2004, as part of Hotelympia, an annual catering trade exhibition that began in 1936. The only stipulation for the participants, working in teams of three, was to prepare a three-course meal fit for a club chairman and his VIP guest – in a time 15 minutes short of the full 90. Ten clubs entered the contest, including Aston Villa, Bolton, Liverpool, Manchester United, Reading and West Ham United. Norwich City were notable absentees.

Meanwhile, the long-time rivalry between Manchester United and Manchester City extended to the corporate hospitality front in 2004. Historically, the Reds had always been the market leaders, having grown their business from a £100,000 turnover in the mid-1970s to a £2 million profit in 2002–3 under managing director of catering Mike Whetton.

But City seemed about to steal a march on their red rivals, with their arrival in the City of Manchester Stadium with its purpose-built hospitality facilities. These enabled City to increase their meal supply from 1,800 at Maine Road to 3,000. The stadium could also offer better conference and exhibition facilities for use on non-matchdays than its antiquated predecessor, with such high-profile companies as Glaxo, Asda and Manchester Business Enterprises having sampled the City of Manchester Stadium in its first season, in preference to United.

And you can still buy Bovril, which always seems to be hotter than tea or coffee. The clubs, particularly those playing in the upper echelons, have made efforts to improve their catering facilities but, even though the earth may be charged, the service can sometimes be a little haphazard. Queues inevitably form shortly before kick-off and at half-time, and there is evidence to suggest that, at some grounds at least, home fans are treated rather better than those of the visiting team. At Old

Shrewsbury Town's burger bar at Gay Meadow, a ground they wish to leave. *Northdown*

Trafford, for example, Manchester United supporters are able to buy refreshments with relative ease, whilst visiting fans may have to queue for a quarter of an hour to buy a beer.

Only a few years ago, you could buy a perfectly edible meat pie from a pie shop near Bolton Wanderers' Burnden Park ground for as little as 25 pence. Competitions were held amongst younger supporters, to see who could eat the most (the record is believed to be seven). Today, a slightly larger factory-made pie will probably set you back a couple of pounds and a bottle of factory-made beer is likely to cost the same. At the other end of the scale,

Shutters are closed during play at Forest Green's Lawn to prevent alcohol consumption in view of the pitch. *M. Heatley*

clubs with restaurants attached will sometimes charge exorbitant prices for very ordinary meals. Even the prawn sarnies available in executive boxes have been known to curl at the edges. A few club restaurants are however really quite good. Norwich City had a reputation for providing some of the most disastrous football refreshments in the country, but then TV cook Delia Smith, a long-term supporter and now a director of the club, took a hand. A new range of delicacies is now on offer (see page 125 for more on Delia's culinary revolution.

A few other clubs have recently been awarded points for their gastronomic efforts. The Cleethorpes and Grimsby areas have long been noted for their excellent, and cheap, fish and chips, and the fish and chips available at Blundell Park itself are very good. Derby County's Pride Park offers value-for-money refreshments (the mushy peas are reputedly full of flavour), whilst Hillsborough serves soup with granary bread and Portman Road does an excellent cold collation.

Former Fulham hero Gordon Davies (left) poses with super-fan Jim Sims before his matchday duties as a dining-club host. *Northdown*

Commentators' Cuisine

BBC TV football commentator John Motson has bad memories of a Wembley snack which once turned an England international into a 90-minute battle with his stomach. 'Before the match, Trevor Brooking went for hot dogs and I got the teas in. Within minutes of biting into the hot dog, I had a serious stomach upset,' he said. 'I don't remember anything about the match, but I do remember the stomach upset. It lasted for days afterwards.'

The late, great Kenneth Wolstenholme recalled going hungry during his most famous broadcast, the 1966 World Cup Final at Wembley. 'In those days the BBC paid us a pittance and they thought we didn't need food. In the 1966 World Cup Final we had some cold ham and chicken at a briefing meeting before the match, but once we were inside Wembley stadium there wasn't anything at all, not even a cup of tea at half time.'

Wolstenholme also pointed out the pre-eminence of lower-division facilities in the football food pecking order as evidence that top clubs were now interested only in the corporate hospitality game. 'Football is now divided into two stratas and the top strata thinks that football is no longer the ordinary man's game and only wants the people who can afford a three-course lunch and a bottle of wine in the executive restaurant.

'I have been very distressed in recent years to see football slip away from the grassroots and the people who really count, the ordinary fans.'

Leave it to Delia

Norwich City's culinary activities have certainly benefited from the input of Delia Smith who, with husband Michael Wynn Jones, effectively owns the club thanks to a £4 million cash injection in 1996. A cool £2.5 million a year is raised by her conference and catering facilities, half of which significantly occurs on non-matchdays. Themed nights featuring foreign cuisine cooked by chefs from those countries are popular, while the five on-site restaurants each feed an average of 200 people per game. Little wonder chairman Roger Munby says, 'It's a godsend to have Delia on board.'

On the more proletarian front, Norwich have invested in their own pie ovens, and bake 4,000 every Saturday. The lower costs that have resulted through bringing this in-house mean more revenue for the club. The catalyst for this seems to have been Mark Sullivan, a life-long Norwich fan who considers himself to be a pie connoisseur. He bumped into Delia at the club's last game of the 1999–2000 season and when she asked what the grub was like at Carrow Road replied that the pies were the worst he had tasted!

Future plans for Carrow Road include a hotel on adjacent land, which will be developed on a no-risk profit-share basis, while further land is available for so far undisclosed 'entertainment projects' – this diversification is crucial to a club that registers a trading loss. 'Charlton are a similar-sized club,' says Munby, 'but they have a turnover of £35 million...ours is £13–14 million. We can achieve the same, and we're going to.'

The influence of Delia Smith has turned Carrow Road into a gastronome's paradise. Its pre-match eateries include the Gunn Club (above), Jarrold Top of the Terraces (far left), Delia's Bar (left) and the Board Room.
NCFC

The Football Food League Table

The most recent comparison of football food came in 1998 with the publication of the *Colman's Football Food Guide*. There will have been many changes since then – apart from new entrants to and dropouts from the League, Delia Smith's Norwich will doubtless be in the fast-food Premiership – but at the time of writing this remains the last word.

Interestingly, lower division clubs dominated the football food league, while the national stadium at Wembley was placed an embarrassing 89th in the table. 'The nation's showcase stadium epitomises everything that's wrong with food at football grounds in this country, an awful, over-priced eating experience,' said the guide – a charge Wembley itself understandably refuted.

A team of more than 40 tasters, with a claimed 750 years' worth of football watching between them, cruised the kiosks at 93 grounds including Wembley and between them ate 323 pies, along with 185 hot dogs, 291 burgers and 144 portions of chips. Cambridge proved small can be beautiful, and their commercial manager, Carla Frediani, said the secret of the club's success was their bacon roll – described by the guide as a 'spectacular high spot'. She said, 'We use best back bacon and put two rashers into each roll. The other thing is the smell. If you cook bacon the smell just gets to everyone. I'm a vegetarian but even I get tempted.'

The Balti pies at Walsall, the hot pork rolls at Lincoln City and the pasties at Bristol Rovers were also singled out for praise, while editor-in-chief Jim White voiced several unanswered questions that will be familiar to most supporters: 'Are the staff at food outlets at grounds contractually obliged to be taken by surprise at half-time? Why is the vegetarian option generally confined to a packet of Opal Fruits? What are you supposed to do with your teabag? What's wrong with real milk? Why are the food outlets invariably right next to the urinals?'

Food Football League

1 Cambridge United	24 Bradford City	48 Scunthorpe United	71 Wigan Athletic
2 Huddersfield Town	25 Northampton Town	49 Nottingham Forest	72 Tranmere Rovers
3 Rochdale	26 QPR	50 Crewe Alexandra	73 Stockport County
4 Chesterfield	27 Torquay United	51 Derby County	74 Darlington
5 Charlton Athletic	28 Walsall	52 Blackburn Rovers	75 Port Vale
6 Hartlepool United	29 Fulham	53 Mansfield Town	76 Southampton
7 Rotherham United	30 Blackpool	54 Sheffield United	77 Swindon Town
8 Middlesbrough	31 Leeds United	55 Brentford	78 Manchester City
9 Stoke City	32 Arsenal	56 Plymouth Argyle	79 Chelsea
10 Preston North End	33 Sunderland	57 = Crystal Palace	80 Oldham Athletic
11 Notts County	34 Leicester City	57 = Wimbledon	81 Bury
12 Manchester United	35 Carlisle United	59 Doncaster Rovers	82 Reading
13 Coventry City	36 Luton Town	60 Watford	83 Burnley
14 Lincoln City	37 Barnet	61 Norwich City	84 Cardiff City
15 Ipswich Town	38 Newcastle United	62 York City	85 Peterborough United
16 Bolton Wanderers	39 Macclesfield Town	63 Sheffield Wednesday	86 Tottenham Hotspur
17 West Ham United	40 Aston Villa	64 Portsmouth	87 Chester City
18 Birmingham City	41 Liverpool	65 Exeter City	88 Oxford United
19 Wycombe Wanderers	42 AFC Bournemouth	66 Southend	89 Wembley
20 West Bromwich Albion	43 Scarborough	67 = Gillingham	90 Wrexham
21 Bristol Rovers	44 Hull City	67 = Brighton & Hove Albion	91 Bristol City
22 Millwall	45 Wolverhampton Wanderers	69 Grimsby	92 Swansea City
23 Colchester United	46 Shrewsbury Town	70 Everton	93 Leyton Orient
	47 Barnsley		

Giantkilling Grounds

Each year, when January comes round, top-flight clubs shake in their boots. The reason? The FA Cup third round, when lower-division and even non-League clubs who have survived in the competition thus far have their chance to make their name as giantkillers.

Most big clubs have suffered this ignominy at some point in their history – in recent years Arsenal have been defeated twice, by both Wrexham (1992) and York (1985), Manchester United suffered a shock loss to Harry Redknapp's Bournemouth in 1984 and Everton lost in 2003 to Shrewsbury Town, a club that would lose its League status five months later. It's fair to say that top clubs have increasingly rested players in Cup fixtures, regarding the Premiership as a priority, but the romance of

Shrewsbury's Gay Meadow, seen from the visiting terraces where Everton fans saw their team beaten in 2003. *Northdown*

the Cup remains strong everywhere except perhaps at Old Trafford.

In 1970–1 Colchester United beat mighty Leeds United 3-2, having led 3-0 at one stage of the match. The next season, Hereford United beat Newcastle United 2-1 – and this, it's often overlooked, was after securing a 2-2 draw at St James' Park. Little wonder that when the Magpies were drawn away to non-League Stevenage Borough in 1996 (when the big club was lucky to escape with a 1-1 draw) they did their level best to get them to switch the tie!

Such moves were outlawed by the Football Association after Farnborough Town from the Conference moved their fourth round tie with Arsenal from their own ground to Highbury in January 2003. They gambled that their share of the Highbury gate receipts would exceed the £265,000 offered by Sky for live transmission of the match as originally drawn. In point of fact, anyone familiar with Boro's dilapidated

Above: **Farnborough's FA Cup match against Arsenal in January 2003 was eventually played at Highbury.** *Northdown*

Right and below: **The main turnstiles, perimeter wall and car park at Cherrywood Road all suggest Farnborough would not have been capable of hosting Arsenal.** *M. Heatle/Northdown*

The Greatest Giantkillers

Since the war, only six non-League sides have defeated top-division teams in the FA Cup:

1947–8	Colchester United 1-0 Huddersfield Town (third round)
1948–9	Yeovil Town 2-1 Sunderland (fourth round)
1971–2	Hereford United 2-1 Newcastle United (third round replay)
1974–5	Burnley 0-1 Wimbledon (third round)
1985–6	Birmingham City 1-2 Altrincham (third round)
1988–9	Sutton United 2-1 Coventry City (third round)

Cherrywood Road ground – record attendance 3,581 against Brentford in 1995 – would have been aware that the game could not have been played in safety. And to add insult to injury, the club's manager/owner Graham Westley decamped to Stevenage two weeks later, taking seven players with him and using the estimated £440,000 Highbury receipts to reclaim loans he'd made to the club!

The same stage of the 2003–4 competition saw Conference side Scarborough drawn at home to Chelsea at their McCain Stadium, maximum capacity 6,408. Unable to switch to palatial 42,500-capacity Stamford Bridge, they were happy to accept Sky's offer of a live transmission and, while Scarborough had knocked Chelsea out of the League Cup in October 1989 when the Seasiders were a Third Division club, the priority now was money rather than progress.

Chairman Malcolm Reynolds had saved the club from closure two years earlier, and it had emerged from administration only six months earlier. 'I have spent two years on a daily basis fighting to keep this club alive,' Reynolds said. 'Having been lucky enough to get this far, we clearly owe the town and the supporters their glory day. It is no exaggeration that we've been within hours of not even having a football club and tonight we are talking about Crespo, Mutu, Lampard, Joe Cole. Them coming here just seems unbelievable.'

Chelsea were allotted 1,400 tickets at the McCain Stadium, the capacity of which had been reduced to 5,850 to accommodate the media. While 1,100 paid £25 to sit, the remainder took a trip back in time by standing on the terraces at a cost of £20 (Scarborough usually charge £10 for Conference games). The anticipated revenue from the game included the Sky television fee of £265,000, gate receipts of £50,000 and £50,000 prize money for reaching the fourth round, additional sponsorship and commercial activity bringing the sum to a cool £500,000. This would meet the wage bill for the next two years. 'Managed properly, this money could secure the future of the club for many years to come,' Reynolds said.

Scarborough, who were the first Conference team to be promoted automatically to the Football League in 1987 but were relegated 12 years later, had earned about £167,000 from previous rounds for reaching the last 32 for the first time in their 125-year history. And, with Chelsea winning by just a single goal and surviving a penalty appeal to boot, the Seasiders departed the Cup towards the bank with their heads held high.

Yeovil

Famed giantkillers Yeovil Town hold the record for a non-League club for knocking out the most League clubs (20), but they became a League club themselves in 2003. Their final scalp was Second Division Wrexham, achieving an impressive 4-1 win in a match that was broadcast in several foreign countries, including Romania

Alec Stock was the 29-year-old player-manager at Southern League Yeovil Town when they drew mighty Sunderland at home in the fourth round of the FA Cup in 1949. The Huish Park his club played at had a 10-foot slope from corner to opposite corner, and Stock resolved to use it to his team's advantage. He drew up a plan of psychological warfare that current managers Ferguson and Wenger would be hard-put to equal...and came out of it with a 2-1 win.

'We were not fit to be in the same county as them, let alone on the same pitch. [I] Knew I needed to do something to cut them down to size. I couldn't do it by talking about the

players. The fact that I could get into the team with a dodgy ankle showed how bad we were. So I decided to make our pitch the secret weapon.

'In truth the slope was not that pronounced. I set about making it sound like the bloody north face of the Eiger. To every reporter who came within hearing distance, I said: "Wonder if Sunderland's players have the calves to stand up to our hill?"

'I knew I must be getting through to them because their chairman rang our chairman to ask if the Sunderland players could train on our pitch. I flatly refused, and told our groundsman in the

Alec Stock, manager of Yeovil in their finest hour, in later years.
Ken Coton

hearing of a journalist that "If you see a single Sunderland player set foot on our pitch, take a shotgun to him!"

'By the time it came to kick-off, they were convinced they needed climbing boots. We were a team of part-timers, but it was they who ran out of steam when the game went into extra time. All in the mind, you see.'

'If you see a single Sunderland player set foot on our pitch, take a shotgun to him!'

Roll on 55 years and Yeovil were not only enjoying their very first season in the Football League in their 108-year history but had spent 13 years in a new Huish Park, 'billiard-table flat on an industrial estate that replaced Yeovil's notorious sloping pitch at the centre of the town' as *The Observer* put it.

Sadly, the club's intention to overturn Liverpool in 2004's FA Cup saw them lose 2-0. And the reason can be traced to a pre-match comment by player Paul Terry (brother of England's John). 'This club has an incredible history and you don't have to be here very long to learn about their Cup record. But a lot of their giantkilling over the years was helped by a pitch that sloped steeply and a tiny ground. The minnows that knock out the big teams in this competition often do it on a mud-heap, in cramped conditions and by kicking lumps out of the stars. But Liverpool will be pleasantly surprised because we've got a superb pitch and a modern stadium, with good-sized dressing rooms. We will also be trying to get the ball down and play football against them because that's how we play.'

Barnet

Yeovil's former sloping pitch is rivalled by Barnet's Underhill – but that, like the original Huish Park, is unlikely to survive too much longer. Football League criteria dictate that, if promoted, the club will be given a three-year deadline to cure the problem or face automatic relegation back to the Conference.

This, explains ambitious chairman Tony Kleanthous, would 'put the whole ground out of sync. You would either be watching the game from far above, or underground. It would mean having to knock the whole ground down.' Further to this, Underhill's 5,500 capacity meant the Bees could not be promoted to the Football League until the required minimum capacity was reduced from 6,000 to 4,000 in summer 2003.

The combination of measures offers the club a lifeline but has also accelerated Barnet's drive towards a new stadium. 'We have a tiny non-League ground for what is considered to be a big club by the rest of the Conference. We've been caught in a timewarp, watching other clubs catch us up and pass us by. Trying to come up with decent facilities for the people of Barnet has become a dirty word.'

The club's plans for a 10,000 all-seater stadium to the south of Underhill were scuppered by Barnet Council in 2002 because it encroached into three acres of Green Belt land occupied by Barnet Cricket Club. Since then they have come up with no alternative to the South Underhill scheme, but the news they could play League football at the existing

ground, albeit temporarily – 'the best news we've had in eight years…it has bought us time' (Tony Kleanthous) – may have caused a thaw in relations. The council 'will investigate finding new land for Barnet, but we do not have the finances for it at the moment,' he continued. 'If I'm asked to compete with Tesco to buy every site that becomes available then no, there won't be a site for us in the borough. But if the council views us as important and worth retaining then I'm certain the council can find us a site. I have spent nearly 10 years here and I will carry on until I find a solution. I will either die, go broke, or find a solution.'

'We've been caught in a timewarp, watching other clubs catch us up and pass us by.'

Kleanthous greeted the good news of the temporary lifting of the restrictions to Barnet entering the league by opening his chequebook to make general improvements on the ground, emergency access being one of the key issues. 'The immediate pressure is off. I will be investing £1 million into (Underhill) over the next few years,' he said in late 2003.

The team showed positive reaction to the news by reaching the Conference play-offs in 2004 despite the loss of manager Martin Allen to Brentford.

Hereford

Hereford United, then of the Southern League, had been playing in the FA Cup since 1924 and reached the first round proper for the 21st successive time in the 1971–2 season, when success in a second replay against Northampton won them a third round tie against mighty Newcastle United at St James' Park. While this game is seldom remembered, the Bulls had the temerity to go ahead in the first minute, though it took a late goal from player-manager Colin Addison to earn the part-timers a draw.

The mudheap of a pitch at Edgar Street levelled the teams still further, but as the tie headed into its last five minutes the First

Division side was ahead. Ronnie Radford picked up a return pass from Owen and burst the net from fully 35 yards. Ricky George's extra-time winner finished off the demoralised Magpies, and Hereford were the first non-League club to conquer a top-division side since 1949.

History rarely records what happened next – largely because, having drawn another member of the elite in West Ham, Hereford could do no more than draw 0-0 in front of another capacity Edgar Street crowd, losing to a Geoff Hurst hat-trick in the replay. The Hammers were not to be so fortunate the following year, however, when the third round draw paired the teams once more. The Bulls beat West Ham 2-1 at Edgar Street (after a 1-1 draw at Upton Park) before losing tamely at home to Bristol City in round four.

Edgar Street had registered its record crowd of 15,526 in an FA Cup game against Newport County in 1950, failing to add any Football League club's scalp to that of Scunthorpe United secured in the first round. Exeter City

2003 found Hereford United once again a non-League outfit, three decades on from their historic victory over Newcastle. Edgar Street hadn't changed much either. *Northdown*

were beaten in 1953–4 and Aldershot in 1956–7, but it was the following season's 6-1 demolition of Third Division (South) side Queens Park Rangers that still stands as a record for a non-League club against a League club in the FA Cup.

Brighton, Hartlepool and York have also been beaten at home by Hereford, and Leicester held to a draw, in the years since they again dropped out of the League – entry to which was facilitated by their Newcastle win.

Wimbledon Then

Plough Lane, London SW19, was Wimbledon FC's spiritual home from just before World War 1 until the club was moved lock, stock and barrel to Selhurst Park in 1991. Built on disused swampland on the corner of Haydons Road and Plough Lane, where a refuse site had once stood, it was a homely ground incorporating a pub (The Sportsman) and a night-club (Nelson's) where the 'Crazy Gang' used to make merry with supporters after yet another unlikely win.

That top-flight football was played in such unlikely surroundings now seems improbable, but it was. Former owner Sam Hammam claims he had submitted plans for a 12,000 all-seater stadium to the local council in 1978

but been turned down. He also spent £500,000 on a proposed stadium at Wandle Valley that also, he says, failed to receive approval. He held onto the Plough Lane site from 1991, when the club vacated it, until 1998 when he sold it to supermarket giant Safeway after leaving the club.

There are those who say a 25,000-seat stadium could have been built there, as Hammam owned adjoining land that had been a gypsy camp. They also say that two sites, Wandle Valley and the Tanden Works, had planning permission but both permissions were allowed to lapse.

Surprisingly, only two of the games on the way to Wembley in 1988, those against West Bromwich and Watford, were played at Plough Lane, but many a scalp was claimed on home turf in League matches, notably Arsenal, then Champions in 1990, and Tottenham, beaten 5-1 in 1991. These games stand as highlights of the 79 years Wimbledon FC spent at Plough Lane, London SW19.

Wimbledon Now

The club's long-awaited move to Milton Keynes Hockey Stadium from its Selhurst Park 'lodgings' in 2003 did not meet with universal approval. The rump of disaffected support had already moved to Kingstonian's Kingsmeadow ground, there to form non-League AFC Wimbledon, but BBC Five Live commentator Jonathan Pearce was similarly unimpressed with what he found when commentating on his first game at Milton Keynes. 'The stadium is not suitable for football. Tidy, neat and run by a small team, it's a security nightmare – too many open spaces to provide a battleground for the ill-intentioned hooligan.'

Above: **A derelict Plough Lane survived for several years after the football team moved away. Owner Sam Hammam sold it to a supermarket chain.** *Neil Presland*

Below: **Fans turn their back on play on 21 April 2002, the last game of Wimbledon's season.** *Neil Presland*

Overleaf: **Wimbledon's, now MK Dons, new home at Milton Keynes has yet to witness any giant-killing performances.** *Robert Lilliman*

Let There Be Light

Early Days

When you consider that the Football League did not sanction the use of floodlights until the mid-1950s, it is quite remarkable to note that the first British football match to be played by artificial light took place almost 80 years earlier. The use of electricity was still in its infancy, but someone had the bright idea of using it to stage an evening game at Bramall Lane, Sheffield, between two representative teams from that city. The floodlights were powered by dynamos, which were in turn driven by two engines situated behind each goal. The lights themselves were attached to wooden towers, and just before the kick-off, they were hauled up to a height of 30 feet (a little over 9 metres).

The Sheffield experiment had its detractors, but most felt that it had been a success. The lights were of course focused on the field of play, and this meant that the rest of the stadium was in darkness, and so about 8,000 spectators were apparently able to steal in without paying. They doubtless thought that the experiment was a very great success. The players seemed to like it also, although the lights were at first too bright, and some of the players reported being dazzled by them.

The Victorian age was noted for its many inventions and for the pace of technological change. The floodlighting of sports stadiums was just one more example. It was new and exciting, and it seemed that it would catch on in a big way. Following the Sheffield experiment, a number of floodlit exhibitions were held in various parts of the country. They enjoyed varying success and then, in February 1889, Newton Heath (afterwards known as Manchester United) played Ardwick (Manchester City) under lights at Belle Vue, Manchester. This was a charity event, designed to raise money for the Hyde Colliery Explosion Fund, but this time electricity was not involved. Instead, the organisers provided oil-burning flares which worked quite well, but were later considered to be too dangerous. The burning creosote oil also gave off a singularly pungent smell.

The advantages of floodlighting were obvious, the principal one being that, during the dark days of winter, it would no longer be necessary to bring forward kick-off times in order to ensure that matches were not completed in near darkness. However, at the time, floodlighting brought with it some distinct disadvantages. There were no white balls in those days, and players sometimes had difficulty in locating the brown leather ball under the lights. The organisers tried to get over this little problem by whitewashing the ball, and replacing it as soon as the whitewash wore off. It was not a great success.

The safety of spectators could be a problem (although one suspects that little account was taken of this by those who saw floodlit football as a way of making money) and the reliability of lighting systems was another factor. In 1892, Celtic tried stringing lamps together and hanging them around the pitch, but these seemed to act as a magnet for the doubtless well-intentioned footballers, and a number of the lamps were smashed by flying balls. As the century's end approached, there was a diminution of interest in floodlit football. The odd floodlit game continued to be played, but the Football Association, an organisation which has seldom been ahead of its time, refused to allow lights in all but charity games and friendlies. It was not until after World War 1 that there was a resurgence of interest.

Further Illumination

As technology advanced, floodlights became more reliable. During the years between the two world wars, some football clubs, notably Arsenal and Tottenham Hotspur, began to campaign for their use at League games. They found it very hard going, even though by now floodlighting was widely used at stadiums throughout the world, especially in the United States. Basically, the FA did not want to know and, in 1930, its response to the growing demand was to issue an edict banning all member clubs from playing any floodlit games.

The situation could not continue, and had it not been for World War 2, floodlights would probably have been installed at many League grounds by the early 1940s. However, war did come once more, and professional football largely went into hibernation for the duration. When it re-emerged, and the Football League resumed normal service in 1946, crowds were bigger than they had ever been. The demand for floodlights reasserted itself almost at once, but the FA was determined to hold out for as long as possible.

Following a tour of the USA in 1946, Liverpool returned home to suggest the establishment of a mid-week floodlit league. Both Arsenal and Southampton were interested and it was clear, even to the FA, that the ban would have to go. It was lifted at the end of 1950, by which time a number of non-League clubs had already played matches under lights, the most notable being Headington United. They played a charity game in front of 2,603 spectators on 18 December 1950, with lights borrowed from the exteriors of a number of local buildings. These lights, all 36 of them, were hoisted on top of wooden poles. (Headington later became Oxford United.)

The Headington experiment had attracted the interest of a number of League clubs, and it was not long before some of them installed floodlights of their own. The honour of being the first League club to install lights went to Swindon Town of the Third Division (South). They first lit their ground on 2 April 1951, for a friendly against West Country neighbours Bristol City, and many of the bigger clubs soon followed suit. In October of the same year Southampton, having installed their lights for the then princely sum of £600, became the first League club to play a competitive floodlit game. It was a reserve team fixture, in the Football Combination, and it attracted a crowd numbering 13,654. A couple of weeks later, Arsenal played their annual challenge match against Glasgow Rangers before a massive 62,500 people at a floodlit Highbury.

In Scotland, the first club to use floodlights since those early days, which had seen Celtic players using the lights as targets, was Stenhousemuir. They staged a friendly match at Ochilview Park against Hibernian on 7 November 1951.

The Football League had yet to approve the use of floodlighting for League matches, and it was not until June 1955 that permission was granted for postponed games to be played under lights. Before then, however, Wolverhampton Wanderers, Tottenham Hotspur and Hibernian had all played floodlit games against European sides, and a few FA Cup ties had also been played under lights.

When the Football League decided at last that postponed games could be played under floodlights, little more than a third of League clubs actually had any. Fratton Park was, however, ready for the new era, and on 22 February 1956 it was the setting for the first floodlit League encounter: Portsmouth v Newcastle United. On an exceptionally cold night the venture was deemed a great success by the thousands who turned up, and by many journalists across the country, but there were still a few problems to be faced.

The first of these was that the players themselves decided to emulate their masters at the Football Association, by deciding that they didn't want to play under floodlights after all. Their reasons were simple enough: the maximum wage had yet to be abolished, footballers were not very well paid, and there were worries about the inconvenience of playing during the evenings. Accordingly, the Players' Union instituted a ban on floodlit games but, happily, this was short-lived. The Football League agreed to allow clubs to pay their players a maximum of an additional £3 each for taking part in every floodlit match (what would today's footballers have made of that remarkably generous offer?) and the problem was solved. The League now decided that any match could be played under lights, as long as both teams were in agreement and the lights were of a sufficiently high standard.

Standards did in fact vary considerably, as did reliability: during the late 1950s and early 1960s many a match was plunged into darkness, and it was not unknown for there to be an appeal over the Tannoy system, asking if there was an electrician in the crowd.

Conventional floodlight pylons were always a useful reference point for coach drivers, as in this view outside Bristol Rovers' Eastville, 1971. *Ken Coton*

Nevertheless, by the start of the 1956–7 season, floodlit football could be said to have arrived in earnest.

By 1956, only 38 of the 92 League clubs had installed floodlights, and some of those were well below the required standard. The cost of installation was increasing rapidly – it more than doubled during the 1950s – and many clubs were still reluctant to make the investment. Slowly but surely, however, the lights were going up all over the country, so that by 1960 only two English First Division clubs – Fulham and Nottingham Forest – were without them. During that year, the advent of the League Cup, a competition in which all games were to be played mid-week, caused most League clubs to install floodlights within a season or two.

Towering Achievements

After the earlier experimental attempts at floodlighting, most of the systems installed featured a tower at each corner of the ground, each holding a number of powerful bulbs which beamed their light upon the players below. One distinct advantage of these towers, quite a few of which still survive, is that they guide visiting supporters towards their destination when they are spotted in the distance. One disadvantage is that they can light up the entire neighbourhood, to the considerable annoyance of nearby residents, many of whom feel they have enough to put up with already. The more recent arrival of lights mounted along the edges of stand roofs has helped in this regard, and modern floodlighting is in any case far more sophisticated than it was in the early days. Since the 1970s, floodlighting has also had to take account of the needs of television cameras, especially when colour television first came upon the scene.

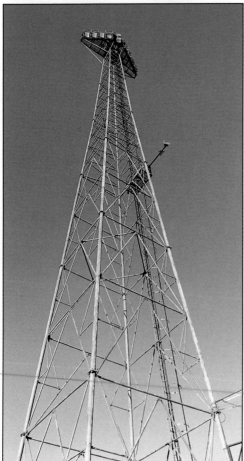

Top left: **Kenilworth Road floodlights, 1970.** *Ken Coton*

Top right: **Stand-mounted floodlights have been widely adopted; Exeter's St James' Park is one example.** *Northdown*

Left and right: **The old and the new: floodlight pylons from Hull's now derelict Boothferry Park (left) and the stand-mounted 'A'-frame lights (far right) at the KC Stadium.** *Robert Lilliman*

The Football Association (having by now probably accepted that floodlit football is here to stay!) has produced guidelines relating to the illumination of the playing surface, and has also concerned itself with 'light pollution' – the spillage of light into the local neighbourhood. When making planning applications, clubs have to undertake a 'floodlight impact assessment' and ensure that the lights are positioned so that they limit light pollution. Meanwhile, the Football League has issued its own regulations regarding floodlights. Regulation 8 (Part 2 – Floodlighting) begins as follows:

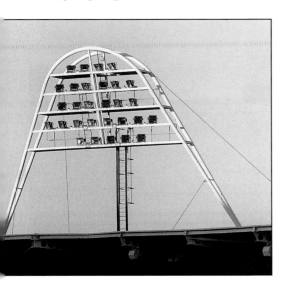

'The average lux value of the floodlights, obtained from 88 readings taken on the grid system provided by The Football League, must meet the following minimum criteria for each division:

	Average lux value	Minimum at one point
Division One (Campionship)	500	300
Division Two (League One)	350	210
Division Three (League Two)	350	210

In order to assess the lux value, a series of 88 readings must be taken with a light meter on a grid pattern set out on the pitch at approximately 10 metres apart. The light meter must be placed on a horizontal plane at pitch level and the average of all the readings is taken to be the average lux value of the floodlights.'

Regulations are regulations but, unless you happen to be an electrician and you know about these things, lux values would appear to be fairly meaningless. One is reminded of soap suds. The Regulation continues:

'The readings must be carried out by a qualified neutral surveyor, a manufacturer or by local electricity boards. The Football League shall require a test certificate and chart to be submitted every two years.

Above: **Bloomfield Road's somewhat squat floodlights fail to rival the famous Blackpool Tower in the background, 1994.** *Northdown*

Right: **Floodlights at Edgar Street, Hereford.**

'Clubs promoted into Division One shall have until 31 May in the first season from the date of promotion to meet the minimum floodlighting requirements for Division One clubs.

'Clubs in Divisions Two and Three must currently comply with the minimum floodlighting requirements for these divisions.

'A new member club entering Division Three must comply with the Football Conference Average Lux Value and has until 1 May in its first Season as a Member Club to meet the Division Three Average and Minimum Lux Value (which, for the purposes of Regulation 8.4, shall be deemed to be the Admission Criteria regarding floodlighting).'

Fascinating stuff, but of course it's necessary. It does, however, seem slightly odd that more light is required for matches in Division One

(now the Coca-Cola Championship) than in Divisions Two and Three (Coca-Cola Leagues One and Two). Are players, and for that matter spectators, expected to have better eyesight in the lower divisions?

New grounds seem to favour mounting floodlights on the stand roof rather than on free-standing pylons, while the non-lattice-style floodlights at smaller grounds are often hinged at their lowest point to enable bulb replacement at ground level, rather than with the use of ladders or lifting vehicles. Floodlight arrays are often also accompanied by mobile phone masts as clubs attempt to maximise every income stream: whether these may one day be found to have an adverse effect on fans or, perish the thought, players remains to be seen.

There is no knowing what the future will hold for floodlighting. It has already spread to cricket grounds, and the lighting at the imposing new or reconstructed football stadiums such as The Riverside, Old Trafford and Villa Park would seem hard, or even impossible, to improve upon. But the march of technology continues and more innovation is sure to follow.

Have a Break

The half-time interval, once a uniform 10 minutes but these days extended to a worldwide 15, is under pressure. And the reason? Clubs want to sell more food and drink! At a FIFA International Board meeting in London in February 2004 it was proposed by German representatives that the mid-game break should be increased to 20 minutes. Studies in that country had concluded that a five-minute extension would mean an increase of at least £200,000 a year in food and drink takings for clubs. Television would also be in favour of the move, since live broadcasts could now include more commercials in the most important break of play.

Surprisingly, perhaps, soccer's supreme rule-making body rejected the proposal on this occasion. FIFA's chief executive, Urs Linsi, said it was clear that the motive was commercial. 'For the players,' Linsi said, 'an extension would be more difficult than easier.' Don't be surprised, though, if this one repeats as often as a badly cooked hot dog.

Swansea City's East Stand, incorporating this futuristic floodlight, was erected in 1981 at a cost of £800,000 to celebrate their rise to the top flight. *Robert Lilliman*

Blues Go Black

Birmingham City owe their survival in the Premiership to the astute management of Steve Bruce and the financial backing of David Sullivan and the Gold Brothers. But events in January 2004 might have led to the suspicion that perhaps the money spent to build a decent team had led to economies in keeping the St Andrew's electric meter fed!

Kick-off of the Blues' FA Cup clash against Blackburn was held up for 35 minutes after the floodlights went out twice. The same thing had happened 12 months earlier when City were at home to Arsenal in a Premier League fixture. Much of the electrical equipment was housed in the ageing main stand, which was set to be renovated once the club established themselves in the top flight.

Bruce said: 'We've all got to look into the delay. It was disappointing. That's three times in total it has happened now – and twice it has happened in 12 months. I'm sure we will look into it and see exactly what happened. We all know the stand is in poor condition, to say the least, but we'll try and review it and do the best we can.'

Referee Paul Durkin eventually allowed the game to get under way at 3.35pm, and Birmingham went on to win 4-0.

Cup Confusion

The same 2003–4 season had seen the half-time team talks in the FA Cup first round tie between Thurrock and Luton Town at the Ship Lane ground in Purfleet delivered in darkness, thanks to a power failure. Since the match was being played before Sky television, the station had brought along extra lights to augment the non-League ground's set-up, and these were deemed sufficient by referee Thorpe to continue the game. Eventually, the power was restored to enable the game to finish as a 1 – 1 draw.

Unfortunately, another floodlight failure occurred at the ground on 27 December, causing the abandonment of the Ryman League derby against Grays Athletic at half-time.

Left: **Huddersfield's new stadium boasts state of the art lighting.** *Abacus*

Below: **Ease of maintenance is important for training facilities.** *Abacus*

Pitches, Posts and Plastic

When the Football Association, in its first official meeting in London in 1863, specified the Laws of the Game, pitch dimensions were laid down but not the nature of the playing surface. Everyone assumed it would be grass. Nor did the pitch have to be either level or in good condition.

While the Premier League will not currently permit grassless pitches – a fact that Charlton Athletic attempted to use in a January 2003 appeal against defeat on a Stamford Bridge 'beach' (see box overleaf) – it's possible that within the next decade we will see the reintroduction of artificial surfaces. FIFA president Sepp Blatter has even hinted that some pitches for the 2010 World Cup in South Africa will be man-made.

The history of artificial pitches in Britain has not been a glorious one. English clubs Queens Park Rangers, Oldham Athletic, Luton Town and Preston North End installed them in the 1980s, with Scottish Third Division club Stirling Albion following suit. Another club north of the Border, Dunfermline Athletic, brought the concept back to British football in 2003 as part of a UEFA-sponsored experiment.

Queens Park Rangers' infamous plastic pitch, the first in the English League, was installed in time for the 1981–2 season, and heralded an era of great on-field success. Second Division Rangers reached the 1982 FA Cup Final, losing to Tottenham in a replay, then romped to the divisional title in 1983. They followed that up by finishing sixth in the pre-Premiership First Division to book a place in Europe and make it to the Milk (League) Cup Final in 1986. All this was achieved under future England manager

Below: **A mid-1990s view of Upton Park shows wear on the pitch.** *Northdown*

Life's a Beach

When Charlton Athletic lost at Chelsea in January 2003, they created history by appealing to the Premier League board for a replay, claiming the grassless Stamford Bridge pitch constituted an artificial surface, contrary to the rules of the Premier League Rule 17, Section 1.

'At no time before the fixture were we informed by Chelsea that we would be playing on an artificial sand surface and not grass,' claimed Charlton chief executive Peter Varney. Premier League rules make no specific mention of grass, only of 'a pitch being of an adequate standard', though they do state that 'no League match shall be played on an artificial surface'. Sand is, presumably, natural. When visiting manager Alan Curbishley raised the matter with referee Mike Dean on the day, the official told him he was only concerned with the fact that the surface might endanger the safety of the players.

Charlton claimed they were put at a disadvantage as they did not have the chance to train on what Chelsea's then manager Claudio Ranieri jokingly likened to Brazil's famous Copacabana beach. 'We were offered no opportunity for our players to train on the artificial surface to judge the effect of the bounce of the ball and to make decisions on the appropriate footwear to be worn in the circumstances,' said Varney.

'Chelsea officials advised us that their players trained on the pitch on Thursday and Friday and the footwear worn by them was appropriate for an artificial surface. The footwear worn by some of our players was not appropriate for the surface.' Varney added that his club was advised by Chelsea that the surface was the base on which their new pitch would be laid the following week.

'Based on information provided by Chelsea officials, we have reached the conclusion that, in the interest of the integrity of the Premier League and sportsmanship between member clubs, we must lodge a formal complaint. In the light of the evidence available we are requesting that the match be replayed on a grass surface.'

Chelsea said in a statement: 'The referee and match officials carried out an inspection of the pitch before the game. Their decision was that the surface was in a satisfactory condition for the match to be played.'

Charlton's case, believed to be the first of its kind, was heard and rejected by a three-man Premier League board comprising chairman Dave Richards, chief executive Peter Scudamore and secretary Mike Foster. After receiving submissions from representatives of both clubs and match referee Dean, the inquiry deemed that the result should stand.

A pristine pitch at Stamford Bridge in 2004, miles away from the playing surface that upset Charlton the previous year. *D. Heatley*

Terry Venables, the man who coincidentally or otherwise once wrote a book called *They Used To Play On Grass*.

But was it El Tel or the advantage of the plastic pitch that got them there? Keeper Peter Hucker, who preceded David Seaman in the side, says the latter – but years later still feels the effects: 'It was a huge advantage to the team. We just changed our game according to

Above left: **A worn goalmouth at Tamworth's Lamb ground betrays the demands of a long season.** *Northdown*

Left: **Cardiff's Ninian Park pitch looks the worse for wear – and sand – in March 1972.** *Ken Coton*

the weather. I never got beaten by a dodgy bounce, but my knees bear testament to how flaming hard it was!'

Though artificial grass promised playability in all weathers and no cancelled matches, QPR's pitch was nearly put out of action when vandalised the night before a televised home game. The perpetrators were protesting the innocence of one of their friends who was about to go to prison: not content with slogans, they even stole the centre spot. The ground staff at Loftus Road had to work through the

The exact height of the crossbar is laid down in the rules of the game but there have been a few mistakes: as recently as 1989 it was discovered that one of the crossbars at Portsmouth's Fratton Park ground was an inch lower than the other.

The elliptical goalposts of today have largely replaced the more traditional squared-off wooden posts of yesteryear, though Scottish clubs stayed with square posts for many

Advert for Brodie's goal nets from an early Cup Final programme.

years. In 1920, a Mr J. C. Perkins of the Standard Goals company in Nottingham persuaded local team Forest to try the much stronger elliptical shape.

Elliptical posts and bars are now used around the world, though there have still been several incidents of broken posts over the years. In 1981 Chester City's goalkeeper Grenville Millington collided with a post, and the whole lot fell on top of him. He was largely unhurt, but the match had to be abandoned. On another occasion, Brentford's Chick Brodie tried swinging from the crossbar in an attempt to clear a cross. The bar broke, and once more the goal was destroyed.

Until the 1980s, most posts were made from wood, Douglas fir generally being the preferred choice. In recent years, however, aluminium or steel goals have replaced them, ground staff finding maintenance a lot easier. Apart from this, the goalpost has basically remained unchanged for over a century.

One John Alexander Brodie, a Liverpool engineer, is said to have invented the goal net, calling it 'a huge pocket', and nets began to be used from January 1891. The first footballer ever to 'put the ball in the back of the net' was Fred Geary of Everton at a trial game in Nottingham. (The referee, incidentally, was Sam Widdowson, the man who invented shinpads.) Brodie, whose engineering works graced Britain, Spain and India, always claimed goal nets were his finest achievement.

Certainly, the presence of a net prevented many a future dispute, although it didn't rule out the possibility of the ball crossing the goal-line, hitting a stanchion at the back of the goal, and rebounding back into play with no goal awarded. A referee's lot is seldom a happy one.

Groundsmen

The men and women who look after our football grounds are largely unsung heroes. We have all seen the groundsman pottering around the pitch at half-time, replacing the occasional sod which has come adrift during the first period of play, but most spectators do not give his job a second thought. Not, at least, until the pitch becomes unplayable, whereupon everyone starts to blame him.

A groundsman's lot is not always a happy one. In Britain, the vagaries of the weather

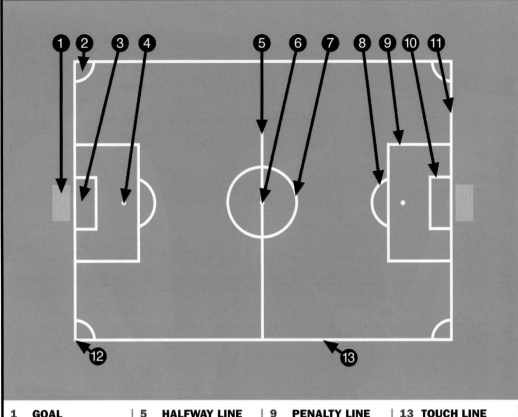

1	GOAL	5	HALFWAY LINE
		9	PENALTY LINE
		13	TOUCH LINE

<table>

1	GOAL	5	HALFWAY LINE	9	PENALTY LINE	13	TOUCH LINE
2	CORNER ARC	6	CENTRE SPOT	10	6-YARD-LINE		
3	6-YARD-BOX	7	CENTRE CIRCLE	11	GOAL LINE		
4	PENALTY SPOT	8	PENALTY ARC	12	CORNER		

Pitch Markings

When the Football Association formed in 1863, pitch markings were not specified in any detail. The pitch could measure up to 200 yards (180 metres) in length and up to 100 yards (90 metres) in width, flags marking the four corners. The goalposts were set eight yards (7.32 metres) apart, a measurement that has remained constant ever since. The current minimum and maximum pitch dimensions are: length 100–130yd (90m–120m); width 50–100yd (45–90m).

The rules were revised in 1891 and specified the provision of goal lines and touch (side) lines, plus a centre circle, the goal (six yard) areas and a line 12 yards from the goal from which a penalty kick (introduced the previous year) could be taken at any point. An 18-yard line across the almost full width of the pitch was also introduced to denote the penalty area.

1902 saw the current pitch layout completed with a halfway line, goal areas, penalty areas and a penalty spot. The one and only further change came in 1937 in the shape of the penalty arc, a suggestion from various European football associations.

Corner flags are a necessary accessory to mark the boundaries of the playing area. Regulations state that there must be four corner flags, but nothing about their shape, size or colour. *Northdown*

mean that groundsmen are engaged in a constant battle to keep football pitches in good condition. These days, they are of course aided by modern technology, and their duties include the maintenance of plant and equipment and, where applicable, maintenance of undersoil heating and drainage. The marking out of the pitch prior to a game is also their responsibility, and during the summer the turf has to be treated and cut and, in places, relaid.

There is a variety of college courses and training schemes for youngsters wishing to take up a career in groundsmanship, and the value of the job is becoming increasingly recognised. Mike Appleby, the Football Association Leagues Manager, stated in 2003 that: 'The FA recognises the vital importance of groundsmen because without them there would be no games, no players and no matches. Quality pitches are essential for the development of the game at every level. Poor

'Today groundsmen are respected as never before and our work is under the spotlight all the time. The pressures are greater but at last we are being recognised for the crucial role we play in sport. Without us football could not be televised – and that has seen a major change in the way our profession is regarded.'

Roy Rigsby, winner of the 2003 IOG SALTEX Groundsman of the Year Award

Ground staff attempt to fork in excess rainwater to ensure the game is played. *Ken Coton*

Undersoil Heating

The postponement of any fixture due to a frozen pitch is a costly and time-consuming business, especially at Premier League level. Loss of revenue is the main problem, especially with corporate hospitality and catering involving considerable non-recoupable expense. Equally unwelcome is the administrative hassle and disruption to the fixture list.

An under-pitch heating system is one solution. Tottenham Hotspur's system comprises an underground network of over 18 miles of plastic pipework laid 18 inches below the pitch surface. A uniform 35° Celsius is selected when the system is set for snow; temperatures range downwards dependent on the weather. 'Hard frost', 'frost' and 'minimum' are the other options. They check the efficiency of their system with a thermal imaging camera.

Rolls of insulating material can help keep out a heavy frost. *M. Heatley*

playing facilities can seriously hamper this development, and continued participation by players at all levels.' Stating the obvious, perhaps – but at least he said it. He went on to say that: 'Groundsmen often have to do the work single-handed and normally for no reward: much of their work is voluntary, for small clubs.'

The Institute of Groundsmanship, which was founded in 1934 and covers ground maintenance in all its manifestations, has for the last two years presented awards to football groundsmen. In 2003, Roy Rigsby of Manchester City, a former crown green bowler who had begun his career with Blackburn Borough Council 28 years earlier, collected a silver salver and cash award for being named IOG SALTEX Professional Football Groundsman of the Year. Awards were also made to groundsmen from Football League and major non-League clubs, thus recognising the value of the contribution made by ground staff everywhere.

IOG SALTEX Groundsman of the Year Awards 2004:

Premier League:
Dave Roberts – Southampton

Division One:
Alan Ferguson – Ipswich Town

Division Two:
Dave Brown – Hartlepool United

Division Three:
Mark Patterson – Macclesfield Town

Highly Commended
Premier League:
Paul Burgess – Arsenal FC
Roy Rigsby and Lee Jackson – Manchester City

Division One:
Richard Eastham – Preston North End
Wayne Nash and Paul Wilkins – Cardiff City

Division Two:
Marcus Cassidy – Swindon FC
Mark Williams – Wycombe Wanderers

Division Three:
Ian Dowler – Cambridge United

Club Shops and Souvenirs

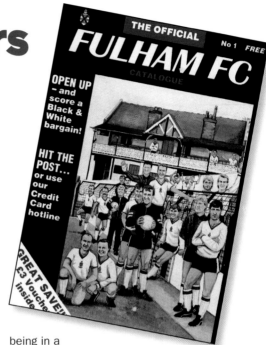

Next to refreshments and corporate entertainment, club shops are the aspect of football grounds that has been subjected to the most serious upgrading in recent years. Previously, clubs sometimes took over the lease of a small shop for the sale of souvenirs, and often this was situated at a distance from the ground. Today, you are much more likely to find a large, well-fitted emporium either built into the stadium or, as at Celtic Park, situated within the stadium complex.

Continental-style club superstores, like the one at Barcelona's Nou Camp, now abound, and one can buy anything from a ballpoint pen to a full replica kit. At a price. Football has come of age as far as merchandising is concerned, and youngsters up and down the country are thankful for it, even though their parents may be rather less pleased. There is no doubting the fact that 'ordinary' people

being in a position to afford such luxuries is a good thing, but equally there can be little doubt that football clubs, if they continue to charge higher and higher prices, are in serious danger of killing the goose that laid the golden egg.

Programmes and Memorabilia

Between the wars, most League programmes were priced at either one penny (c0.5p) or twopence (c1p). In 1933, even the likes of Manchester United and Arsenal were charging only twopence. Programmes were far from being the glossy magazines of today, but a typical black and white one would contain about 16 pages and would provide reasonably comprehensive, if somewhat biased, information concerning the latest goings-on at the club. Generally speaking, they were well

Top: **Fulham FC catalogue, 1987.**
Author's collection

Left: **Replica shirt revenue is a crucial component of any club's revenue, and West Ham United are no exception.** *Northdown*

155

This page: **Club programmes remain the first and most regular purchase of most supporters. Here is a selection from non-League clubs.** *Author's collection*

Right: **The 1897 FA Cup Final programme. Aston Villa beat Everton 3-2 at Crystal Palace.**

CRYSTAL PALACE.

Saturday, April 10th, 1897.

FINAL TIE

FOR THE

CHALLENGE CUP of the FOOTBALL ASSOCIATION.

ASTON VILLA.

Colours—
Claret and Light Blue Shirts,
White Knickers.

Goal.
WHITEHOUSE.

Backs.
SPENCER. EVANS.

Half-Backs.
REYNOLDS. JAMES COWAN. CRABTREE.

Forwards.
ATHERSMITH. DEVEY. CAMPBELL. WHELDON. JOHN COWAN.

Forwards.
MILWARD. CHADWICK. HARTLEY. BELL. TAYLOR.

Half-Backs.
STEWART. HOLT. BOYLE.

Backs.
STORRIER. MEECHAN.

Goal.
MENHAM.

Colours—
Blue Shirts, White Knickers.

EVERTON.

Referee—J. LEWIS (Lancashire). Linesmen—J. HOWCROFT (Redcar). A. SCRAGG (Crewe).

Official Programme. ONE PENNY.

Two's Company

At Italy's San Siro Stadium, shared by Milan teams AC and Inter, the shop has a 'red side' and a 'blue side'. Things weren't so simple at QPR's Loftus Road, however, where, for the two seasons from 2002 to 2004, the shop did double duty as Fulham's matchday emporium – a situation that required a finely tuned military-style operation to work efficiently.

The QPR shop would trade until five o'clock on the Friday evening. If Rangers were at home the following day, nothing moved. But if Fulham had a game, the staff would have an hour to remove all the blue and white stock from the shelves before the arrival of a container from a Harrods warehouse up the road at Osterley, Middlesex. And though the procedure became quicker with practice, arranging the Fulham merchandise for the morning was still a four- or five-hour job.

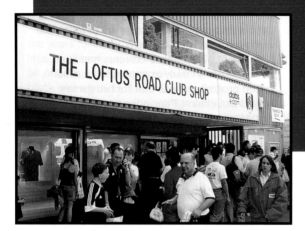

Fulham's shop staff would return to the premises at nine on Saturday morning, giving themselves an hour to iron out any snags before opening their doors at ten. The shop remained open for an hour after the full-time whistle, after which the container arrived and the procedure was reversed!

Fulham's temporary club shop at Loftus Road, 2004. *M. Heatley*

7p. By the mid-1980s League programmes typically cost anything between 30 and 70 pence (in 1986, a Manchester United programme could be had for 40p) and although few, if any, colour photographs were included, they were beginning to take on the appearance of today's 'matchday magazine'. Wolverhampton Wanderers provide a good example of the changes that were afoot. Even though they were languishing in Division Three, in 1988 they were producing an excellent programme, with colour photographs, for 70p.

By now, sales and marketing strategies were also much more in evidence. Football programmes had long advertised the sale of lapel badges, hats (Fulham would sell you a 'Home-made Ski Hat' for the equivalent of 32.5p in 1962) and autograph books, but by the 1980s the range of goods on offer was much wider. In addition you could sponsor various items of an individual player's kit – for example, £35 for a Barnsley player's boots or £12 for his 'Shorts and Stockings' – and you could also buy full replica kits for upwards of £20.

A new ground demands a megastore, and St Mary's is no exception. *M. Heatley*

With more and more people owning cars, travel to away games increased in popularity, but for those not wishing to drive, the clubs (or supporters' clubs) usually provided a coach or three. This was normally very inexpensive. In 1986–7, Notts County fans could travel to Chesterfield for £3 or to Bolton Wanderers for £4. Supporters were certainly on the move – and so were their football clubs. It would soon cost you a great deal more to follow your team.

Give Them Credit

Visitors to certain football grounds may have found a leaflet pressed into their hands advising them that not only could they buy club merchandise, they could now get a club credit card to help pay for it. But there is a league table of interest rates that should be consulted first: in February 2004, for instance, Arsenal's Classic credit card charged a 17.9% rate on purchases, while rivals Manchester United's card was a full 2% cheaper at 15.9%.

Such cards often entitle the holder to a discount when buying club merchandise: Charlton Athletic are particularly generous in giving the holder a £30 voucher to redeem in the club's store when they first use the card.

Top and left: **Selling programmes and merchandise – official and otherwise – outside Stamford Bridge.** *D. Heatley*

A humble Portakabin supplies the fans of Forest Green Rovers. *M. Heatley*

elsewhere in this book) which have risen sharply. With those old twopenny programmes now rebranded as glossy full-colour matchday magazines, priced at up to £3 (the 2003 FA Cup Final programme cost £8.50), the cost of souvenirs of all kinds has gone through the roof. Admittedly, the choice of goods has expanded considerably and you may still be able to buy a metal badge for a pound or two, or an autograph book for just a little more. However, if you want to buy a sleepsuit (complete with club crest) for your infant, you'll probably be asked to pay at least £12 and, when the child grows older, a T-shirt will cost twice as much. At the top end of the market, a replica shirt is likely to cost at least £30, even though price-fixing has, in theory, been abolished.

The Premiership clubs do normally reduce their admission prices when playing teams from the lower leagues in cup competitions, a fairly recent example being at Goodison Park where Everton charged a maximum of £15 for a League Cup game against Stockport County, but it is not only admission prices (dealt with

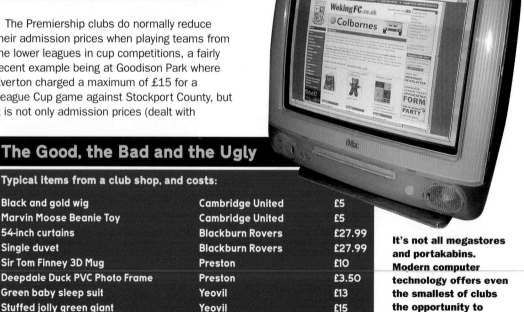

The Good, the Bad and the Ugly

Typical items from a club shop, and costs:

Black and gold wig	Cambridge United	£5
Marvin Moose Beanie Toy	Cambridge United	£5
54-inch curtains	Blackburn Rovers	£27.99
Single duvet	Blackburn Rovers	£27.99
Sir Tom Finney 3D Mug	Preston	£10
Deepdale Duck PVC Photo Frame	Preston	£3.50
Green baby sleep suit	Yeovil	£13
Stuffed jolly green giant	Yeovil	£15
Mobile phone cover (Nokia)	Bournemouth	£20
Paper block (note pad) holder	Bournemouth	£7.50

It's not all megastores and portakabins. Modern computer technology offers even the smallest of clubs the opportunity to upload a website and sell their merchandise via the internet. *PHD*

Stadium Svengalis and Benefactors

Football's Money Men

A lot of loot has been put into football in recent years. This chapter outlines the careers of the major players on the investment front.

Top of the list, as far as overall personal wealth is concerned, is the owner of Chelsea Football Club. Just 36 when he bought the club, Roman Abramovich is a remarkably young billionaire. He initially made his money in oil (aluminium and meat processing were also involved) during the economic chaos which afflicted Russia following the fall of communism, and is reputed to be worth £3.8 billion – although estimates do vary and the figure could be considerably higher. In the year 2000 Abramovich was elected Governor of the province of Chukotka in northeast Russia, and has since poured money into the region. He has put quite a bit into Chelsea, too. It cost him about £150 million to buy the club, and he has spent well in excess of £100 million on players. Ken Bates remained as chairman until March 2004, even though he received almost £18 million from the sale of his shares to Abramovich.

Although he is no longer on the board of Tottenham Hotspur, Hackney-born Sir Alan Sugar, who made much of his money from personal computers, still has a substantial stake in the club. His total assets are probably worth around £600 million. Elton John is no longer chairman of Watford, but he still has

Chelsea's magnificent Stamford Bridge was rebuilt before the arrival of Roman Abramovich.
D. Heatley

Mohamed Al Fayed, Fulham's benefactor since 1997. *FFC*

The exact origins of the Mohamed Al Fayed millions are shrouded in a certain amount of mystery, but Fulham's Egyption-born septuagenarian chairman has put a good many of them into the football club.

almost 12 million shares in the club. Because of his remarkable spending habits, it is difficult to know just how much he is worth: perhaps about £185 million, although it could all change next week.

The exact origins of the Mohamed Al Fayed millions are shrouded in a certain amount of mystery, but Fulham's Egyptian-born septuagenarian chairman has put a good many of them into the football club. His business interests include the ownership of Harrods and the Paris Ritz, luxury apartments in London, and Kurt Geiger shoe retailers. He owns an estate in Scotland and a very large property in Surrey. In common with many rich men, he also has a number of charitable interests. Although Al Fayed now lives in Switzerland, he has pledged continued support for Fulham and still hopes to build a new stadium when a suitable site can be found. His fortune is probably in excess of £500 million, and he has put about

£80 million into Fulham Football Club.

Dave Whelan, owner of Wigan Athletic, is that rarest of animals – a club chairman who knows about the game because he was himself once a professional. He made his debut for Blackburn Rovers in 1956, but his career was cut short by injury when he was just 23. He bought a grocery store in Blackburn with his £400 compensation and by 1978 Whelan's Discount Stores was sold to the Morrison supermarket chain for £1.5 million. Whelan then paid £7,400 for J. J. Bradburn's sports shop in Wigan, known locally as 'JJB'. He expanded the business under the name of JJB, opening new shops in towns across the country. In 1994 the company was floated on the Stock Exchange and was valued at £64.5 million. It has had some problems of late, but Whelan and his family are estimated to be worth something in the region of £300 million.

David Ross was part of a consortium led by Gary Lineker, set up to rescue Leicester City in 2002. Due to the fact that Leicester were in administration following relegation from the Premiership, his initial investment was a paltry £250,000. The resurgent Foxes have, however, cost him a lot more since. Ross made his money when he co-founded the Carphone Warehouse and he is currently estimated to be worth in excess of £300 million. Gary Lineker's fortune is estimated at about £7 million.

John Madejski, the chairman of Reading Football Club, was once a local newspaper

Above: **The JJB Stadium's predecessor, Wigan's Springfield Park, pictured in 1983.** *Robert Lilliman*

Right: **Reading chairman John Madejski has every reason to be proud of the stadium he built and named, which opened its doors in 1998.** *www.readingfc.co.uk*

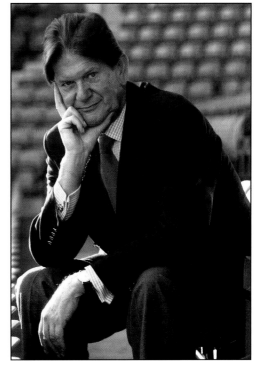

sales executive. He went on to make his millions via the *Autotrader* publications and has since branched out into numerous other business ventures. He became Reading's chairman in 1990 and he later funded the new £40 million stadium. Madejski's arrival upon the scene was wonderful news for Reading fans – Robert Maxwell once held 33% of Reading's shares, and he had wanted to merge the club with Oxford United. Madejski is thought to be worth approximately £260 million.

Tanzania-born Firoz Kassam, the owner of Oxford United, was ranked 19th on the UK Asian Rich List in 2003. Kassam came to this country as a 19-year-old in the 1970s, and later opened a fish and chip shop in Brixton, London. He encountered a few financial problems in the early days, but once those were sorted he did rather well. He now owns a chain of hotels, including the magnificent Heythrop Park, which is set in 450 acres of parkland in Enstone, Oxfordshire. His current fortune is estimated to be in the region of £90 million. This is not a great deal by the standards of some, but it's a pretty good result for someone who came to this country as a more or less penniless teenager.

Darlington's ex-chairman, George Reynolds, was born in Sunderland. He is famous for having had a criminal record, but all that is now in the past. Having decided to go straight, he started up a company making kitchen worktops. His factory was gutted by fire in 1994, but it was rebuilt and in 1999 he sold part of the company for £40 million. He rescued Darlington from probable oblivion in the same year, and went on to build a new stadium. Reynolds has a somewhat acerbic nature, and did not take kindly to journalists and other writers delving into his early life and criticising his chairmanship of the football club. This being so, it must be said that he did wonders for his football club, even though Darlington later went into administration and Reynolds resigned as a director in January 2004. His estimated worth is currently in the region of £40 million.

Sir Jack Hayward spent an estimated £74 million in his attempts to get Wolverhampton Wanderers into the Premiership. Born very close to Molineux, Sir Jack made his first fortune selling tractors in the USA and he then engaged upon business interests in the Bahamas. The investment in his beloved club at last paid off, when Wolves were promoted to the Premiership in 2003. It has, however, been something of a struggle for them since and although Hayward has now withdrawn from the club, which was relegated from the Premiership at the end of the 2003–4 season, his son Jonathan remains involved.

Lebanese businessman and former civil engineer Sam Hammam bought Wimbledon Football Club for £100,000 in 1981. Under his chairmanship the Dons rose to Premiership status, and 'Sam the Man' was loved by one and all in London SW19, for a while. He later moved the club from Plough Lane to Selhurst Park, to groundshare with Crystal Palace. It was a decision which was to have unfortunate repercussions for a club with a small fan base. Hammam later sold his shares in Wimbledon, mostly to two Norwegian businessmen, and then bought Cardiff City for a little over £3 million. He has to date spent a further £10 million on the Bluebirds. Hammam is now worth about £40 million.

The owner of Norwich City Football Club made her money by writing. Delia Smith, until recently Britain's most popular cookery writer and broadcaster, and the person largely responsible for a resurgence of interest in the art of preparing meals, owns the only League club in Norfolk. She is possibly worth a mere £20 million, but her influence has been tremendous – especially as far as the catering is concerned. She has enormous enthusiasm for the game, and for her club, which is worth about £7 million. Apologies to Delia for including her in a chapter otherwise devoted to 'Money Men'.

Norwich City director Delia Smith. *NCFC*

Birmingham City owe their opulent St Andrews ground and Premiership status to directors David Gold (left) and David Sullivan (above).

Roy Smiljanic – BCFC

Who Are You?

A number of investors in football clubs like to keep a low profile. Joseph Lewis is a foreign exchange dealer who keeps a very low profile indeed. His company, ENIC, has a stake in a number of football clubs, including Glasgow Rangers and Tottenham Hotspur. Another low-profile man is Trevor Hemmings, who could well be worth more than £700 million. He is a former bricklayer, who made his millions in the gaming industry, and he has financial interests in Preston North End, Charlton Athletic and Bolton Wanderers.

Dermot Desmond is probably almost as wealthy as Trevor Hemmings. He is a former stockbroker and a non-executive director of Celtic, and he owns a large stake in Manchester United. Meanwhile, Malcolm Glazer, who made his fortune in American shopping malls, has also built a substantial stake in United. Together with horse racing multi-millionaires John Magnier and J. P. McManus, Glazer substantially increased his shareholding in the club/company during 2003, fuelling speculation that a takeover was imminent. Another racing man, Harry Dobson, owns about £40 million pounds' worth of shares in Manchester United, while Dutchman Jon de Mol has a 4% holding.

Jack Walker was the high-profile chairman of Blackburn Rovers until his death in the year 2000. He put £100 million into the club but his younger brother, Fred, still lives in Blackburn and is involved with the club. The family, of which Fred is now the head, is reckoned to be worth about £650 million.

Birmingham City have a couple of directors who are each worth up to £500 million: chairman David Gold and director David Sullivan together have a controlling interest in the Blues.

More Big Investors

David Murray, former chairman and still a major shareholder in Glasgow Rangers; Jack Petchey of Aston Villa; Polys Haji-Ioannou, a 9% shareholder in Tottenham; and Brett Warburton, vice-chairman of Bolton Wanderers, are all thought to have personal assets worth at least £200 million. Brian Kennedy, chairman of Stockport County; David Moores, chairman of Liverpool; Paul Gregg, a director of Everton; Danny Fiszman, a leading shareholder at Arsenal; Michael Sherwood, a director of Watford; Sir Tom Farmer, majority shareholder at Hibernian; Sir Richard Storey, a non-executive director at Sunderland; and Milan Mandaric, the Yugoslavian-born owner of Portsmouth, all seem to be worth at least £100 million.

There are many other multi-millionaires who are involved, to a greater or lesser extent, with modern day football. Many of them are really quite poor when compared to those noted above, but a few of the better known gentlemen are:

Theo Paphitis, Ryman Group chairman, who rescued Millwall in 1997 and, by way of making economies, later charged his players 50 pence each for their breakfast toast.

Ron Noades, the former chairman of Crystal Palace and then Brentford. Noades, who also fancied himself as a manager, still owns Brentford but is no longer chairman.

David Dein, the current vice-chairman of Arsenal, whose shareholding is worth about £15 million.

Max Griggs, who made his fortune by courtesy of Doctor Marten and his boots, and who created Rushden and Diamonds in 1992 prior to selling out in 2004.

Paul Madeley, a playing legend at Leeds United, who is a major shareholder at non-league Halifax Town.

Freddie and Bruce Shepherd, brothers who between them have an £11 million investment at Newcastle United.

Doug Ellis, once ousted as chairman of Aston Villa, but now back again.

Bill Kenwright, the former *Coronation Street* actor turned theatre impresario and chairman/part owner of Everton.

David Sheepshanks, a food producer who is chairman of Ipswich Town.

Superstitions

Footballers are notably superstitious, and the pre-match rituals of even the most strait-laced players have become the stuff of legend. From Paul Ince emerging last and shirtless from the tunnel to Peter Schmeichel 'closing' his goal by kicking both posts, they've taken their place in modern folklore.

It's probably not surprising, then, that superstitions have attached themselves to grounds with similar potency, if not regularity. We'll take a look at a number of case studies – some surprisingly modern – that suggest

Was Southampton's futuristic St Mary's Stadium dogged by an old-fashioned Pompey curse? *M. Heatley*

witchcraft in football is not confined to the ball skills of the likes of Thierry Henry and Cristiano Ronaldo.

When Southampton had built their new St Mary's Stadium in 2001, they were understandably keen to register a win. Their difficulty in doing so was initially ascribed to the lack of the 'fear factor' which had been instilled in opponents by The Dell, their home for the previous 113 years, where the crowd was literally within arm's length of the pitch. Eventually, though, a more sinister explanation emerged.

When local South Coast rivals Portsmouth rebuilt the stand at the Fratton End of their ground in 1997, a Saints-supporting builder

had left his 'good wishes' indelibly etched in the concrete. It was then suggested that builders who followed Pompey had, in retribution, buried one of their own club's shirts, not to mention a blue and white scarf, at the ground in a bid to scupper Southampton's success.

'Legend has it that Sir Bevois has vowed to protect us against all invaders and I'm sure that would include Pompey fans'

A commendably unworried Nick Illingworth, of the Southampton FC Independent Supporters' Club, claimed there was a benevolent spirit at work at the stadium, built on an old Saxon site. Sir Bevois, the knight after whom the nearby Bevois Valley district was named, had long ago been hailed as the city's protector after slaying a dragon, and Nick was happy to recruit him as the Saints' spiritual guardian. 'Legend has it that Sir Bevois has vowed to protect us against all invaders,' said Illingworth, 'and I'm sure that would include Pompey fans. Workers at the new stadium have reported ghostly goings-on in the night so perhaps our ancestors are protecting us.' The fact the ground was on the site of an old graveyard may also have been relevant.

The *Daily Echo* reported that the Pompey shirt was swiftly dug up by vigilant Saints supporters after the Portsmouth-based sub-contractors had knocked off for the day. Southampton chairman Rupert Lowe dismissed the Pompey plot as 'puerile' and said tight security would ensure nothing else could be buried beneath the turf. Of the scarf, however, we've heard nothing more...though Saints' luckless run ended with four consecutive wins.

Just as Southampton went three and a half months before their first St Mary's win,

Dedicated paving stones at St Mary's Stadium, Southampton, include a 'lucky stone'.

fuelling superstition, so the Millennium Stadium which had opened two years earlier produced a string of 'one-sided' games to suggest it possessed a jinx of its own. The Welsh national team failed to win in their first six matches at their spectacular new home, while the divisional play-offs, LDV Vans and FA/League Cup Finals also threw up an astonishing sequence. The clubs who won the right to play there could have been forgiven for not bothering to turn up after they were allocated the south changing room.

Twelve teams – Arsenal, Chelsea and Manchester United among them – had consecutively tasted defeat playing with their fans at that end of the stadium. The unlucky streak encompassed rugby, too: Swansea, Ebbw Vale and Neath all lost after emerging from the 'fated' changing room.

Feng shui experts who visited the stadium recommended the dressing rooms be painted in bright red, yellow and orange colours, and these were duly incorporated by Andrew Vicari, one of Wales's top artists, whose 7-foot high mural of a sun, a galloping horse and a phoenix now adorns the wall of the so-called 'room of doom'.

Millennium Stadium officials were keen to play down the talk of a jinx. Stadium manager Bob Evans said before the 2002 promotion play-offs: 'The Stadium offers a level playing field, in all senses of the phrase, to every team that plays here. In reality there is no physical difference between the two dressing rooms and it is only a matter of time before this statistical anomaly is broken. But this is the greatest venue in the world and we are prepared to go to

any lengths to ensure that all teams enjoy their Millennium Stadium experience.'

Stoke were the team to rewrite history when they beat Brentford 2-0 to secure promotion to the First Division. Manager Gudjon Thordarson was determined to use the so-called curse to his advantage, telling reporters before the match: 'I'm very confident that that will be broken. Some of the players might be worried, but I'm going to turn it into my favour and our favour, so we take our players down there and change the spirit inside the dressing room.' The artist, who was there to witness the victory, said that Stoke 'were the better team but I think I can claim some credit for banishing this losing streak once and for all'.

Vicari's work brought more luck than that of a feng shui expert who was brought in during March 1992. Nottingham-based Paul Darby carried out a feng shui blessing, involving bells, incense sticks and sea salt, in a bid to counterbalance the 'bad spirits' in one end of the giant stadium ahead of the LDV Vans Trophy final. But when Cambridge lost 4-1 to Blackpool after using the unlucky end, Dr Darby blamed negative energy from a media room in the stadium.

Streaks have been known to work the other way too, albeit very rarely. Brighton's temporary move to the Withdean athletics stadium after their sale of the Goldstone Ground has seen them register more than one impressive unbeaten run: 14 games between November 2003 and May 2004 was the backbone of a successful promotion push. It was just reward for fans who'd followed the Seagulls to Gillingham for two depressing seasons.

Derby County were founder members of the Football League in 1888 and moved into the Baseball Ground seven years later, in 1895. It was to be their home until the 1997 relocation to Pride Park. Their feat in reaching the FA Cup finals of 1898, 1899 and 1903 seemed noteworthy until the fact they had been unsuccessful on each occasion was linked with them having had to evict gypsies who had been camping on the Baseball Ground site. Had one of its former inhabitants left a curse behind?

A 1903 FA Cup Final against Bury suggested as much, but an injury to County's keeper during the match provided a more plausible excuse. That said, those with long memories revived the story in 1946 when Derby reached their fourth Cup Final after regularly losing at the semi-final stage. Club captain Jack Nicholas was left with little option but to cross a gypsy's palm with silver in an attempt to lift the curse. It seems to have worked as the Rams beat Charlton Athletic to take the Cup back to Derby for the first time – though, in a spooky postscript, the match ball burst not only during the Final but again in their next League match – also versus Charlton – five days later!

Third Division Oxford United ran up against a cross between Southampton's and Derby's hoodoos when they moved into the Kassam Stadium in 2001. Such was the newly relegated outfit's poor form in its £15 million home, that the club's chairman called in the Bishop of Oxford, no less, to exorcise it! The bishop, the Rt Rev Richard Harries, had reportedly been summoned because gypsies were said to have cast a curse after the club went to the High Court to evict them from the site of the new stadium, their old camping ground. The farmer who originally owned the land had allowed gypsies to stay in return for helping him with harvesting and haymaking.

Club chaplain the Rev Michael Chantry, who contacted the bishop after United lost in 13 of their previous 17 League games, said: 'You could regard it as an old wives' tale, but Oxford United's history of bad luck this season speaks for itself. The bishop is an enthusiastic supporter. He sprinkled holy water on the pitch, said a prayer of exorcism, and blessed the new stadium.'

Chairman Firoz Kassam was rather more prosaic, as chairmen often are: 'Now the manager can't blame the gypsies if we don't start winning more matches. The bishop has done his bit, now it is up to the players to do theirs.' A spokesman for the bishop said: 'Hopefully, Oxford United will now feel they are playing on a level spiritual playing field, as well as a level grass one.' The ceremony was enacted by the bishop, resplendent in a purple cassock, on the pitch before Oxford's home clash with York City, which, for the record, ended in a 2-2 draw.

However, this was far from the end of the matter. Due to excessive media interest on what was clearly a slow news day, the bishop was forced to issue a statement denying any exorcism element, insisting the ceremony was purely to bless the stadium. His spokesman, Richard Thomas, told BBC Radio 4's *Today* programme the 'curse' was not the reason for the visit. He said: 'What the bishop did was what many clergy do, which is bless the ground. He used a prayer which said "Bless this place and protect it from evil."' The Rev Michael Chantry swiftly fell into line: 'I don't want to give the impression I'm a great believer in gypsy curses, but I think to say prayers of blessing in a positive way is a better way of putting it than lifting a curse.' Quite so.

Another example of holy water was sent in the post to Coventry, vainly fighting for their Premiership lives in 2001. It was accompanied by a note instructing manager Gordon Strachan to sprinkle the water on the centre circle at Highfield Road before the Liverpool game.

As manager of the Sky Blues, and a notably unconventional soul to boot, Strachan might have been expected to have had faith in the concept of heavenly intervention – instead, unpredictable as ever, he declined the offer and threw the bottle away. 'I'm grateful for someone taking the trouble to send it to me,' he said. 'I'd thank them personally but I can't read the writing on the letter. Although I'm not particularly religious, I don't think we are quite in the league of needing miracles yet.'

As it happened, the 2-0 reverse against the Reds was a sign Coventry's 34-year stay in the top flight was about to end and with it Strachan's somewhat shorter reign as gaffer. He would resurface, of course, at a thoroughly de-spooked St Mary's Stadium!

Like Strachan, Barry Fry is known as one of the more extrovert characters in football, with his touchline ranting and penchant for industrial language. During his days as Birmingham City manager in the 1990s, he went to greater lengths than mere exorcism to lift a curse on the St Andrew's ground, but found little success.

Fry, desperate to get his sleeping giant of a club into the Premiership, was prepared to try anything, including painting the soles of the players' boots red. But while watering the pitch (and the stands) had proved important in World War 2 when part of the ground was set alight while the stadium was being used as a temporary fire station, Fry was not about to call the fire brigade. His next solution was both natural and more ingenious.

'This guy, who was an expert on such things, told me that if I peed in all four corners of the ground that would get rid of it – not that it's an easy thing to do,' he said. 'It's a pretty difficult exercise, to squirt a little by the corner flag, walk 60 yards to the next corner and do it again – four times in quick succession.

'And it didn't work: I still got the sack,' said Fry, now manager and owner of Second Division Peterborough. It's not noted whether his players were less keen to volunteer for flag-kick duties after the ritual...nor what the St Andrew's groundsman thought about it!

As a not so serious postscript, the *Oxford My Oxford* website reported in 1998 that their local team's manager Malcolm Shotton was set to follow Fry's example by ordering his players to urinate on different parts of the (pre-Kassam Stadium) Manor Ground pitch to exorcise an evil spell he believed was the cause of recent poor form. The plan backfired, however, claimed the website, tongue-in-cheek, 'when striker Kevin Francis was told to urinate in the goal mouth. Sadly, he sprayed it over the crossbar.'

Swansea, who were battling to avoid a second successive relegation and a slide to the League's basement (Third) Division in 2001, called in their own 'voodoo experts' to lift their cursed results sequence after spoon-bending psychic and sometime Exeter City director Uri Geller had detected 'evil influences' at the South Wales club's Vetch Field home. But instead of a spiritual presence, an African dance act was engaged to do the business.

'This guy, who was an expert on such things, told me that if I peed in all four corners of the ground that would get rid of it – not that it's an easy thing to do,'

Quite why the Kenyan Boys, who were touring nearby with the Cottle & Austen circus, volunteered to come to Swansea's rescue is uncertain, but Swansea communications manager Peter Owen was not going to look a gift horse in the mouth. 'They've asked to help out and so we invited them to come along,' he said. 'When Uri Geller visited us a while ago he said there were black spirits at the club. He even claimed these spirits caused the suicide of one of our players, Tich Evans, who played here in the 1920s.'

The corners of St Andrews in which then Birmingham manager Barry Fry (above) relieved himself to get rid of a curse.
Roy Smiljanic – BCFC/www.theposh.com

Unfortunately, heavy rain forced the voodoo dancers to stay under cover and, without their essential input, the club, whose supporters were simultaneously hoping for a big-name financial buy-out, failed in their bid to avoid the drop. As one despairing fan memorably posted on their message board, 'We're an absolute laughing stock – Uri Geller, the Kenyan Boys, Black Spirits, Chris Evans, Catherine Zeta Jones, Tom Jones…when's it all going to end? Like most fans, I've reached the point where I don't even feel angry, 'cos there's literally no hope any more.' Call the Samaritans, someone!

Overseas, football superstitions run even stronger than here, with Argentina a noted hot-bed. Not content with the standard 'lucky pants or shirt' ritual followed by many fans, the Rosario team once brought a witch to the stadium to help protect their goal. Racing, a team from Buenos Aires, organised a religious pilgrimage complete with priests in 1998, to change their luck.

There are also South American rituals to bring bad luck to opponents. Racing fans, when not on pilgrimage duties, bring sugar to throw onto the pitch when they play city rivals Independiente, while Boca fans used to bring chickens into the stadium when they faced River Plate: this unique example of fowl play is now forbidden.

Two of Tanzania's biggest clubs were reportedly penalised in late 2003 for performing 'juju' witchcraft rituals before a clash, the African country's Football Association taking a dim view of Simba and Yanga's antics. 'These are our biggest clubs and their strong beliefs in witchcraft can set a bad example for upcoming teams,' said Mwina Kaduguda, the secretary-general of the Tanzanian FA's interim committee. 'We have fined both teams $500 and we are also going to start a campaign to educate all the teams in the League that juju has no place in football.' It seems that after Simba placed a 'substance' on the pitch at half-time, two Yanga players 'neutralised' it in Barry Fry fashion.

Again, though, Argentina could claim to be leading the way in this field in the person of goalkeeper Sergio Goycochea, who apparently used to hitch up his shorts and urinate on the pitch for luck every time there was a penalty. He allegedly started this practice in the semi-final of the World Cup in Italy in 1990 when it proved effective, so he kept doing it. All attempts to secure a picture of this, however, have been abortive – but if any reader can help, there's always the second edition.

What's in a Name?

As football became increasingly popular during the latter part of the 19th century, many clubs named their grounds after the districts, roads or streets in which they were situated. Examples of such grounds include Old Trafford (Manchester United), Anfield (Liverpool), Bloomfield Road (Blackpool), Elland Road (Leeds United), Filbert Street (Leicester City) and Love Street (St Mirren). There are, of course, many more. In some cases the historical significance of these place or street names is lost in the mists of time, but sometimes it is possible to trace them back to a person of note who lived several hundred years ago, to a geographical feature, or to the previous use of the land. One wonders exactly what went on in Love Street.

England still has quite a lot of lanes, but in the latter part of the 19th century, lanes were almost as numerous as streets or roads. It is hardly surprising therefore, that clubs like Sheffield United, Bury, Notts County and Wimbledon made their homes at Bramall Lane, Gigg Lane, Meadow Lane and Plough Lane respectively.

Football's founding fathers were probably too busy making money and getting their clubs set up to worry too much about the name of the ground. When in doubt, they tended to call it a park, which was reasonable enough in the circumstances. Parks have always been popular, and they were particularly so in the grime-ridden industrial towns in which many professional football clubs were founded. And so we have, or had, Ayresome Park (Middlesbrough), Villa Park (Aston Villa), Brunton Park (Carlisle), Boothferry Park (Hull City), Boundary Park (Oldham), Edgeley Park (Stockport County), and a host of others. The good Saint James was responsible for two football parks: the homes of Newcastle United in the northeast, and of Exeter City in the southwest, both being called St James' Park. In Scotland, the vast majority of League grounds still have 'Park' in their name.

The origins of many other names are fairly obvious. Rotherham was surrounded by mills

St James' Park railway station – but which one? This station serves Exeter's modest ground, not Newcastle United's mega-stadium. *Northdown*

and moors, hence the football club made its home at Millmoor, while Millwall's ground in Cold Blow Lane was named The Den as it was the home of 'The Lions'. Southampton's former home, The Dell, was, in the 1890s, a deep hollow surrounded by trees: in other words it was a dell, except that this particular dell also featured a pond which had to be drained before a football pitch could be laid.

Quite a few football pitches were laid on the site of former rubbish dumps. Hartlepool United's Victoria Ground was one such, located as it was near to the town docks. Constructed in 1886, it was named after Queen Victoria, in honour of the Golden Jubilee, which the ageing

Southampton called The Dell their home from 1898 to 2001. The two-tier terrace behind the Milton Road End, pictured in 1967, had been replaced by a conventional stand by the time of the move. *Ken Coton*

monarch celebrated a year later. The ground was originally used for rugby, but soccer was played there from 1890 and Hartlepool(s) United occupied it from 1908. Lincoln City's Sincil Bank ground was not built on a rubbish dump, but it was named after a drain. Fortunately for the club's supporters, this is not an open sewer but a conduit which runs along the side of the ground from the nearby River Witham, to remove excess water. The conduit is entirely wholesome and really rather attractive in its way.

Amusement parks and other leisure areas were also popular places for the provision of early stadiums. Scunthorpe United's home until 1988 was the Old Show Ground. As its name implies, this piece of land was once an old show ground. A variety of events took place there a hundred or more years ago, notably the Scunthorpe Show. Aston Villa's ground stands on the site of the mid-Victorian Aston Lower

Grounds Amusement Park, Wrexham's Racecourse Ground, having previously had a reputation as a place of drunken debauchery, had later been a site for charity shows and other decorous entertainments, while Wolverhampton Wanderers' Molineux once had pleasure gardens, a boating lake and a cycle and athletics track. Wolves' ground was named after a local family, whilst the Pittodrie Stadium, the home of Aberdeen, was named in honour of a local worthy who lived in the village of Pittodrie, some 20 miles northwest of the city. Supporters of Aberdeen will tell you that there is no truth in the rumour that, in the ancient Celtic language, pittodrie meant a 'place of manure'.

There was probably little going on in the way of entertainment at Swansea City's Vetch Field in the 19th century (Cardiff supporters will probably tell you that there hasn't been much going on since, either). Vetch is in fact a species of plant, which is also known as tare. It obviously grew where Swansea's ground now stands, but The Vetch Field was also known as the Old Town Ditch Field. The ground at which West Bromwich Albion play, The Hawthorns, seems to have fostered plants of a more spiky

nature, whilst Shrewsbury Town's Gay Meadow was so named because, before the advent of Shrewsbury Town Football Club, the field was a favourite spot for fun and games. It just goes to show how the English language evolves. On the east coast of Scotland, Arbroath's Gayfield perhaps had similar origins.

Spotland was a township, which became part of Rochdale Borough in 1856, hence the name of Rochdale's home. Sheffield Wednesday's Hillsborough ground was originally known as Owlerton, and the club still bears the nickname 'The Owls'. When the ground was constructed, it was well outside the city boundaries but, by 1914, the area was very much a part of a burgeoning metropolis, and had become a part of the parliamentary constituency of Hillsborough. The name of the ground was changed accordingly, but even so the club, known in those days as The Wednesday, did not change its name to Sheffield Wednesday until 1929. Grimsby Town used to be called Grimsby Pelham, and they played at Clee Park. However, they soon moved to Blundell Park, which, as every football fan knows, is in Cleethorpes rather than in Grimsby. The ground was named after one Peter Blundell, who left money to Sidney Sussex College in 1616. The college later purchased land which encompassed the site for a football ground which was to be built almost 300 years later.

A number of clubs have homes which were, at one time, used only for rugby football but Derby County's former home, the Baseball Ground, was indeed once used for baseball. Francis Ley, a local industrialist, laid out the ground during the 1880s for the use of the workers. Mr Ley later visited the United States, and returned full of the joys of baseball. He encouraged the American game in Derby and he had some success – the club had its own baseball team for a time – but in the end football prevailed.

AFC Bournemouth, Walsall and Cardiff City all had grounds named after their benefactors. Cooper Dean let some wasteland to Boscombe FC in 1910 and two years later Bournemouth and Boscombe Athletic became a professional club. Bournemouth still play at Dean Court, even though it is now known as the Fitness First Stadium. Walsall's former ground, Fellows Park, was named in honour of H. L. Fellows, a club chairman who had ensured Walsall's survival during times of great difficulty, while Cardiff's Ninian Park was so called after the delightfully named Lord Ninian Crichton Stuart. His Lordship had secured the lease on what was going to be called Sloper Park, and the name of the ground was duly altered.

Tottenham Hotspur had a somewhat less likely benefactor in the shape of a pub landlord. The brewery firm of Charringtons owned the land upon which Tottenham's White Hart Lane pitch was eventually built. The landlord of the nearby White Hart pub was keen that a football pitch be constructed on the site and, thinking of the profits to be made from thirsty supporters, he apparently talked the Tottenham directors into approaching the brewery about providing such an amenity. Charringtons had intended to build houses on the site, but they agreed instead to rent it out to the football club.

Other London grounds have interesting origins, and none is perhaps more unusual than Fulham's Craven Cottage. The original cottage, built in 1780 by the sixth Baron Craven, stood on land which had once formed part of Anne Boleyn's hunting grounds. It was used as a hunting lodge by George IV, and Edward Bulwer-Lytton wrote his famous tome *The Last Days of Pompeii* within its walls. The cottage burned down in 1888 and when Fulham Football Club took over the site in the mid-1890s it was overgrown and thoroughly neglected.

Although West Ham's home is usually known as Upton Park, its official name is The Boleyn Ground. The name was taken from a nearby

Right: **Tottenham Hotspur's White Hart Lane ground has had more brewery links than their one-time Holsten sponsorship.** *Robert Lilliman*

Below: **Cardiff's Ninian Park, seen here in 1986, reflected the generosity of a benefactor.** *Robert Lilliman*

house, built in 1544, and because it had turrets it was known as Boleyn Castle, after Anne Boleyn. Charlton Athletic's ground is known as The Valley because it was originally a derelict chalk pit, which looked like a valley after excavations to turn it into a football field had been completed.

The New Stadiums

There is a recent vogue, which some people dislike intensely, for naming stadiums after the football clubs' main sponsors. It is the way of the commercial world and supporters will probably just have to get used to it. We now

Above: **Boothferry Park, Hull's home since 1946, was showing the strain by the end of the 20th Century.** *Robert Lilliman*

Right: **Hull's 25,500-capacity Kingston Communications stadium opened its gates in 2002.** *Robert Lilliman*

have, amongst others, Bolton Wanderers' Reebok Stadium, Leicester City's Walkers Stadium (a crisp name if ever there was one), Dumbarton's Strathclyde Homes Stadium and Bradford City's Bradford & Bingley Stadium. The latter is of course named after the building society, but it does at least have the merit of sounding like a proper local name, as indeed does Southampton's St Mary's. But how many people outside Southampton know that the club's magnificent new arena is officially called the Friends Provident St Mary's Stadium? One club that abandoned its new name after a few years was Huddersfield. Their McAlpine Stadium is now known as Galpharm Stadium.

The previously mentioned Fitness First Stadium, home to AFC Bournemouth, may perhaps serve to inspire the team during training sessions and, just possibly, Hull City's players will co-ordinate their on-field activities with more precision at their Kingston Communications Stadium. Some clubs content themselves with naming stands or other specific areas of the ground after their modern day benefactors. Blackburn Rovers have their Jack Walker Stand, named after the man who

Wycombe Wrangle

Ground-naming rights are a new phenomenon in UK sport but have already been a source of considerable controversy. And when Wycombe Wanderers FC renamed their Adams Park the Causeway Stadium in summer 2003 the floodgates opened to a storm of criticism totally out of proportion to the Chairboys' average home support of 5,500.

The deal, worth 'a significant six-figure sum over the next three years', was unpopular with traditionalist fans, who found an ally in club director Alan Parry. 'I'm uncomfortable with the idea,' he said, 'but having access to the club's finances I know how important this deal is to the club. The decision was taken for the best possible motives. It is a positive step to improve the club's finances. My wish is that in three years' time the club's finances will have improved to such an extent that we will be able to revert to Adams Park and keep the name for ever.'

In defence of the club, its shirt sponsor had withdrawn in mid-agreement thanks to a change in corporate ownership that triggered a clause in the agreement – so a short-term fix was necessary. 'This is not a decision that was taken lightly,' chairman Ivor Beeks added. 'It went to two or three board meetings before a decision was made. At the end of the day, we are here to make sure that the football club survives. It was a financial decision and we needed to make it.'

In response to supporters who felt the heritage of the club had been not only undervalued but damaged, Beeks claimed that he could gauge the feelings of the late Jack Adams, son of Wanderers' greatest benefactor, Frank Adams. Beeks, who joined the Board six years after the death of Frank Adams, told the Bucks Free Press: 'I've been involved for 14 years on the board and for 13 years I sat on the board with Jack Adams. I knew him exceptionally well and I'm reasonably sure in my mind that if he knew the situation, Jack's considerations would have been the same.'

London Wasps Rugby Union club, tenants of Adams Park from the 2002–3 season onwards after Fulham displaced them from Queens Park Rangers' Loftus Road, were given an estimated £10,000 to alter their notepaper and advertising materials to reflect the change of name.

Wycombe's first ground, Loakes Park, had been gifted to the club in 1947 by former player Frank Adams, who negotiated with owner Lord Carrington for

The gates to Adams Park, the name by which most fans wish to continue calling the ground, according to a recent survey. www.chairboys.co.uk

put millions into the club, but Scunthorpe United very nearly deserve a prize for cramming in as many sponsors as possible: All four of their seating areas bear sponsors' names – County Chef, Scunthorpe Evening Telegraph, Don Cass Community and Caparo Merchant Bar Stands now grace the stadium at Glanford Park.

A few new grounds have escaped the names of builders, banks and building societies. Having spent 80 years at Maine Road, where a

crowd of 83,260 once watched a League game, Manchester City's new ground is known simply, and elegantly, as the City of Manchester Stadium. Known at first as Eastlands, the stadium was built for the 2002 Commonwealth Games, City moving in during August 2003. Sunderland's Stadium of Light may not, as names go, sound very original, but it does convey a degree of much needed hope for the future. The name was also chosen for a good reason. The ground is built on the site of the former Monkwearmouth Colliery and its gates bear the legend 'Into the light'. These words formerly appeared on a sign at the top of the colliery, so the stadium, which also features a giant miners' lamp, honours the former pit workers.

the freehold a couple of years earlier. The club then played in the Isthmian League. In his speech to the crowd at the match celebrating the gift, Frank Adams said 'If future generations obtain the same enjoyment out of Loakes Park as it has given me in the past, then this gift will have been worthwhile.' Frank Adams died shortly after his 90th birthday in 1981 but one of his sons, Jack, was heavily involved with the ground relocation negotiations that led to Wycombe's move to Adams Park in August 1990. The ground was, fittingly, named after Wycombe's main benefactor.

Executive Director Rod Tomlin declared the Causeway deal 'a very welcome one from the club's point of view. Sponsorship in various different guises is a necessary and important ingredient in the business of a professional football club...However, we have had to balance the financial benefits against the various sensitivities associated with the name change. We have certainly not taken this lightly, but I believe we will be able to demonstrate over time that this new association has positive benefits for the Club.'

As an olive branch to fans, outraged by the change of name, the Woodlands Stand was renamed the Frank Adams Stand, the club having originally advertised the stand's naming rights as available for £25,000 per season. Causeway commented: 'We were stirred by the strength of feeling that the fans have shown for the legacy of Frank Adams, and felt it was important to find a way of recognising this. The club has also shown great commitment to the memory of Frank Adams by embracing this initiative.'

Sadly, many felt the affair was a PR disaster, the supporters claiming they had not been consulted on this highly emotive issue. A poll on the club's official site was massively (over 90%) in favour of keeping the name. The poll on a fan site www.chairboys.co.uk attracted a four-figure response to the question 'Should the Adams Park name be dropped for less than £100,000 per year?' and had the following three options:

1. Yes – Every little helps and it doesn't matter how we get it – 21% response;
2. No – Our heritage counts for far more – 56% response;
3. Unsure – I want to hear the figures officially from the Club – 23% response.

Northampton Town's Sixfields Stadium, to which they moved from the County Ground in 1994, and Middlesbrough's Riverside Stadium are nice and straightforward, but some Scottish clubs are even more down to earth: Hamilton Academical used to play at Douglas Park, but they now play at New Douglas Park.

Other grounds, while not bearing the name of a sponsor, simply bear the name of their owner or chairman. Hence, Reading's magnificent Madejski Stadium, conveniently situated just off the M4 motorway and named after chairman John Madejski, and Oxford United's Kassam Stadium, named after the club's owner Firoz Kassam. Dave Whelan did not name Wigan's ground after himself when he became chairman. Well, not quite. Having

made his fortune with JJB sports shops, he decided to call Wigan's new home the JJB Stadium. How long will it be before other multi-millionaire or billionaire chairmen resist the temptations of immortality? Will Fulham one day play at the Al Fayed Pyramid Stadium, or Chelsea at the Roman Abramovich Oil Fields Arena? We shall see.

Lasting Memorials

Owners come and owners go, and so for that matter do players and managers, but it is the players and managers who will always be remembered – especially those who made a significant contribution to their clubs and to the game in general. Until fairly recently, most great footballers lived simply in the memories

Middlesbrough's Riverside Stadium opened for business in 1995, with naming rights accorded to Cellnet. *Robert Lilliman*

of supporters, memories jogged from time to time by occasional ancient black and white photographs in programmes, or by snippets of grey and white film shown on television, often when a footballing great had just died. In recent years, however, many clubs have seen fit to immortalise their former heroes by the erection of permanent memorials.

Statues have become popular. Amongst those erected to date, Ipswich Town have one of England and Ipswich manager Sir Alf Ramsey outside their Portman Road ground, Leeds United have Billy Bremner with arms akimbo at Elland Road, and Manchester United have one of their outstanding manager, Sir Matt Busby. Stoke City boast a statue

The Memorial Ground, Bristol, is true to its name by commemorating the dead of two World Wars. *Robert Lilliman*

of the most famous footballer of them all – Sir Stanley Matthews, while Liverpool, always a little different, honour Bill Shankly with the Shankly Gates on Anfield Road, as well as with a statue to the great man. Middlesbrough's Riverside Stadium has statues of George Hardwick and Wilf Mannion. On a much sadder note, both Anfield and Hillsborough have memorials to those who died in two of football's worst crowd tragedies, while Manchester United have a clock and a plaque in memory of the 1958 Munich disaster.

BILLY BREMNER
1942 - 1997
LEEDS UNITED
1959 - 1976
771 APPEARANCES: 115 GOALS
INSPIRATIONAL CAPTAIN OF THE GREAT
'REVIE' TEAM